G R E E N **B U I L D I N G S** P A Y

GREEN **BUILDINGS** PAY

Edited by Brian Edwards

E & FN SPON

An Imprint of Routledge
London and New York

Published by E & FN Spon, an imprint of Routledge
11 New Fetter Lane, London EC4P 4EE

Simultaneously published in the USA and Canada by Routledge
29 West 35th Street, New York, NY 10001

© 1998 E & FN Spon

Designed by Stephen Cary
Typeset in Gill Sans by Stephen Cary
Printed in Great Britain by the Alden Press, Oxford

British Library Cataloguing in Publication Data
A catalogue record for this book is available from the British Library

ISBN 0 419 22730 X

Contents

Colour illustrations appear between pages 16 and 17

Contents

The authors

Steve Baker is an architect and graduate of the Birmingham and Liverpool University Schools of Architecture. He is a director of Foggo Associates, a multi-disciplinary practice comprising architects, structural engineers, service engineers and quantity surveyors. The practice has a particular expertise in the design of low-energy urban office buildings.

Mel Barlex is a chartered building surveyor, graduate of the University of the South Bank and more recently the University of East London with an MBA. In 1995 he was appointed Head of Property Services for Anglia Polytechnic University where he developed his interest in environmentally conscious building design.

John Beatson trained as a civil engineer at Canterbury University, New Zealand and later as a town planner in the UK. He has held a number of positions in both the public and private sectors in the building and environmental areas. In the 1980s he was Deputy Head of London Scientific Services with responsibility for London's environment policy. For the last nine years he has worked for Cable and Wireless, where he was project director for a number of construction projects, including the Cable and Wireless College. During that time he also developed Cable and Wireless's first group environmental policy.

Rab Bennetts trained as an architect at Heriot-Watt University. After graduating in 1977 he spent 10 years with Arup Associates, before forming Bennetts Associates in 1987. Bennetts Associates have completed a number of award-winning buildings, prominent among which are the low-energy PowerGen headquarters in Coventry, the Heathrow Visitor Centre and the Royal College of Pathologists in London.

Richard Brearley is an architect and partner with John Miller & Partners, London. He studied at the University of Nottingham, has lectured widely on low-energy design and his work has featured in many exhibitions and journal articles.

Brian Edwards is Professor of Architecture at the University of Huddersfield. He trained at schools of architecture in Canterbury, Edinburgh and Glasgow gaining his PhD in 1989, and worked in practice for several years, including a period with RMJM. Author of eight books and numerous journal articles, he is a member of the RIBA Environment and Energy Committee.

Graham Francis is an architect and was at Manchester University. He has been a partner of Sheppard Robson for 14 years and was responsible for the recently completed low-energy Helicon Building in London. He is a member of the British Council of Offices Technical Committee advising on office specification. He manages Sheppard Robson Commercial Group.

William Gething is an architect and was educated at Corpus Christi College, Cambridge. He has been a partner with Fielden Clegg Architects for 14 years and is a member of the RIBA Energy and Environmental Committee. He has a particular interest in environmental issues, IT in constructions and the art of building.

Lennart Grut is an engineer and was educated at Denmark University. He is a member of the Institute of Danish Engineers and of l'Ingénierie Civile de France. He has been a director at Richard Rogers Partnership for nine years and is responsible for projects in Europe and East Asia. He has a particular interest in sustainable issues.

John Gummer, the Member of Parliament for Suffolk Coastal, was educated at Selwyn College, Cambridge, where he was President of the Cambridge Union. After several ministerial positions in both the Thatcher and Major governments, he became Secretary of State for the Environment in 1992 serving until 1997.

Robert Jones was Minister of State for Planning, Construction and Energy Efficiency at the Department of the Environment from 1994 to 1997, and the Member of Parliament for Hertforshire West from 1983 to 1987. He was a member of the House of Commons Environment Select Committee from 1983 to 1994, and sat for two years as committee chairman. Before entering parliament, he was head of research at the National House Building Council.

William McKee is Director General of the British Property Foundation, the trade association which represents the property companies and institutions that form the principal owners and investors in commercial property in the UK. From 1981 to 1992 he was Chief Executive of the London Borough of Merton. Prior to that he was a town planner and transport engineer beginning with the GLC. Later he became Director of Planning and Development, first at the London Borough of Richmond and then at Hammersmith and Fulham.

David Partridge studied architecture at Cambridge University and was a founding partner of Gebler Tooth Partridge, architects. The practice designed office buildings for a number of multi-nations, including IBM, Digital and (For Argent) United Biscuit's group headquarters. He joined Argent in 1990 where he is responsible for master-planning and building design, and has special interest in energy conscious office design.

David Prichard is a partner with MacCormac Jamieson Prichard and was a founding member of the practice in 1972. Energy issues are a special concern of the practice. He studied at the Bartlett School of Architecture, has undertaken energy research for the Building Research Establishment and has been external examiner for RIBA for 14 years. He was partner-in-charge of numerous housing schemes, urban designs and buildings, including Cable and Wireless College, winner of the RFAC Building of the Year award in 1994.

Alan Rowe is a chartered surveyor. He joined MEPC in 1989 and was seconded to Lansdown Estates Group responsible for new building construction at Milton Park, 100-hectare mixed-use business park near Abingdon in South Oxfordshire. He is currently a development manager working on MEPC's industrial property fund.

Ken Shuttleworth studied at Leicester Polytechnic and received a Diploma in Architecture with distinction in 1977. He joined Foster Associates in 1974 while still a student. After an architectural study tour of USA and Canada he returned to Foster Associates in 1977. He was appointed a director of Foster and Partners in 1984 and worked on HongKong and Shanghai Bank where he was responsible for all aspects of the design. In 1994 he received an Honorary Doctorate from De Montfort University.

Peter F Smith received his architectual education at Cambridge University and obtained his PhD from the University of Manchester. From 1986 to 1990 he was head of the Leeds School of Architecture and is now Emeritus Professor of Leeds Metropolitan University. He is currently Professor Associate in the University of Sheffield and Director of the Sustainable Building Network in the School of Architecture. From 1989 to 1997 he was chairman of the RIBA Environment & Energy Committee.

Marilyn Standley is a personnel and facilities manager with a degree in psychology. She is a director of Chesterton Facilities and Property Management. She was Project Director for Addison Wesley Longman. From 1990 to 1994 she has been chairman of the British Institution of Facilities Management.

David Turrent studied architecture at Manchester University and graduated in 1974. He worked in both private practice and local government before setting up ECD in 1980. He is a member of the RIBA Energy and Environment Committee and regularly contributes articles to the architectural press.

Peter Yorke is a classics graduate of Cambridge University who has subsequently worked as a buildings administrator. During his 33 years at the University of East Anglia, he worked on buildings with Sir Denys Lasdun, Sir Bernard Feilden, Sir Norman Foster, Rick Mather, and John Miller and his partner Richard Brearley. He became particularly interested in the process of briefing for buildings required to be elegant, economical, energy efficient and user-friendly.

Acknowledgements

I am indebted to two people in particular for helping this publication to see the light of day with depth and critical perspective. Professor Peter Smith, Chairman of the RIBA's Environment and Planning Committee from 1989 to 1997, gave unfailing support to the two conferences upon which the book is based, and provided encouragement throughout, as well as furnishing a balanced and probing concluding chapter. William Bordass was also a key figure in pointing me towards unpublished data on some of the case studies, and through his own writing helped to establish a rational framework for assessing green buildings.

Many others provided timely and courteous support, not least Barry Lennox of the RIBA Energy Office, Andrew Field of the Department of the Environment, Dave Hampton of the Building Research Establishment, and Richard Grey at the Centre for Construction Ecology.

My task as editor was made bearable by the professional approach and constructive outlook of the chapter authors. They found time to write, comment on, correct and re-correct the chapters based upon their presentations given at the 'Green Buildings Pay' conferences in London and Manchester in 1996. I am particularly indebted to the members of the government who at the time of writing were engrossed in preparations for a general election, yet found time to furnish chapters. It confirms, I believe, that the environment has a calling as compelling as politics.

I wish also to record my gratitude to my secretary at the University of Huddersfield, Karen Beaumont, who tirelessly provided support in the belief that green buildings do pay.

Finally, mention should be made of the financial support from the Department of the Environment, which helped towards the publishing costs and in particular paid for the colour photographs confirming that green buildings pay in an aesthetic as well as environmental sense.

Picture Credits

The author and publishers would like to thank the following individuals and organizations for permission to reproduce material. We have made every effort to contact and acknowledge copyright holders, but if any errors have been made we would be happy to correct them at a later printing.

Figure numbers in **bold** indicate colour illustrations

Photographers

Peter Cook 6.1, 6.2, 6.3, 6.4, 6.5, 6.6, **7**, 8.1, 8.3, 8.4, 8.5, 8.8, 14.3
Peter Durant 3.5
Dennis Gilbert 7.1, **9**, 10.1, 11.1, 11.7, 11.10
Richard Glover 4.8, **5**
Peter Greenland 3.3
Ian Lambot 1.4
Max Logan 14.1
Eamonn O'Mohany 9.4, 9.5
James Morris **4**
Peter Smith 15.3, 15.4, 15.5, 15.6
Anthony Weller 13.5, 13.6, 13.7
Nigel Young 1.8, 7.3, 7.10, 7.11

All other photographs by Brian Edwards

Individuals and organizations

Anglia Polytechnic University 12.2, 12.3, 12.4
Anglia Polytechnic University/BPRU 12.7
Argent Group 5.1, 5.2, 5.3a, 5.3b, 5.4, 5.5
Bennetts Associates 8.2, 8.6, 8.7
BREEAM 1.6, 1.13, 1.14
Cable and Wireless College 1.5, 14.5, 14.6
Carole Townsend 1.10
David Lloyd Jones 1.11
ECD Architects 12.1, 12.5, 15.1
Feilden Clegg 11.2, 11.3, 11.4, 11.5, 11.6, 11.8, 11.9
Fitzroy Robinson & Partners 1.1a, 4.6
Foster and Partners 7.2, 7.4, 7.5, 7.6, 7.7, 7.8, 7.9
John Miller and Partners 13.1, 13.2, 13.3, 13.4
Lansdown Estates 3.3, 3.6
MacCormac Jamieson Prichard 14.2
MacMillan Magazines Ltd 15.2
Ove Arup & Partners 12.6, 14.4
Peter Foggo Associates 1.12, 10.1, 10.2, 10.4, 10.5, 10.6
Richard Rogers Partnership 1.9, 9.1, 9.2, 9.3
RMJM 3.1
Sheppard Robson 1.15, 4.5, 4.9
Short Ford & Partners 2
Studio E Architects 3.4
SVM Partnership 3.2
Wordsearch/Alan Williams 1.14
University of Strathclyde 1.3

Foreword

The Rt Hon John Gummer MP, Secretary of State for the Environment, 1992–1997

There is a growing international scientific consensus that climate change is occurring and that preventative action is necessary. Buildings account for around 45% of carbon-dioxide (CO_2) emissions and are, therefore, a key element in the strategy to combat global warming. Building professionals who have already taken an interest in green buildings can set an example to the rest of the industry and encourage colleagues to realize their environmental obligations. The high level of interest shown at the RIBA 'Green Buildings Pay' conferences held in March and November 1996 reflected the growing recognition among building professionals of the potential benefits of environmentally aware building design and their responsibility to incorporate sustainable development principles into their work.

Green buildings will only result from building professionals working together to achieve this common objective. My department has enjoyed a good working relationship with RIBA over a number of years and I am delighted that, by supporting initiatives such as the 'Green Buildings Pay' conferences and the publication of this book, we have been able to play our part in fostering good working relations between professionals and their institutions. The government is also playing its part in the procurement of green buildings, as demonstrated by the high Building Research Establishment Environmental Assessment Method (BREEAM) ratings given to Eland House and Ashdown House, the Department of the Environment's new headquarters buildings in Central London. Buildings have a long life, and the effects of decisions made now will be with us for decades to come. Low environmental impact should, therefore, be a built-in feature of all building design for teams who claim to be producing a quality product. Quality requires buildings not only to meet the demands of the occupants now but also to be an asset rather than a liability for future generations.

Robert Jones MP,
Minister for Planning,
Construction and
Energy Efficiency,
1994–1997

Green buildings pay: The role of government

The importance of green buildings has never been more central to the economic and environmental welfare of the country. Economic welfare in the sense of creating buildings which are attractive and healthy to use, thereby increasing productivity and keeping company costs down. Environmental welfare in the sense of helping to meet our international obligations on reducing CO_2 emissions and moving towards sustainable development.

The creation of a new generation of low-energy and environmentally benign buildings requires teamwork between professionals. Green buildings are the result of architects and engineers working together using best practice and following the latest guidance from bodies such as the Building Research Establishment (BRE). It is also vital that developers and clients issue to the construction professionals briefs which incorporate high environmental standards. Collaboration between developers and professionals is important not just in terms of the energy parameters put into the building brief but with regard to providing enough time for green design.

The construction industry is at a very interesting time, with new demands from clients for higher environmental standards in the workplace, and new standards on energy-efficiency required of government. Companies are increasingly aware that well-designed buildings improve their image, reduce energy bills and encourage greater productivity.

The role of government is to facilitate and encourage best environmental practice. Buildings have a huge impact upon global welfare, producing about 45% of the carbon dioxide which is de-stabilising world climates. There is little scientific doubt that human activity is responsible for global warming and that buildings are a major contribution.

Buildings are normally designed for a 50-year life, but frequently last much longer. Poorly designed buildings may last for a shorter time and poor energy design is one of the chief factors in premature obsolescence. Since buildings have a long life they influence lifestyles for a considerable period. Development constructed today to poor energy and environmental standards blights future operations and undermines the economic welfare of the nation. We have in the recent past constructed too many buildings which have been poorly designed from an energy point of view and sadly society will have to pay the price for many years. I now detect a return to questions of quality among developers and architects – quality where energy conservation, long-life and low-maintenance materials play a central role. In fact, I became annoyed as minister when design was reduced to a matter of style – quality and style should be seen as complementary.

Besides global warming, governments of all persuasions will be active in raising the environmental performance of buildings. We, with our European partners, are currently phasing out hydrochlorofluorocarbons (HCFCs) in order to preserve the ozone layer. Closer to home, waste is a growing concern: we produce 8 million tonnes of packaging waste a year in the UK, much of this used on building sites. We have set a target of recovering 50% of this waste and directly recycling 15% of it by 2001. Architects need to design for waste minimalization and developers should incorporate the Eco-Management and Audit Scheme (EMAS) into the

development process. They could set an example by specifying materials which carry the EMAS logo thus ensuring that waste is effectively reduced on the building site. Waste is not only a question of lost resources but lost energy as well, and finding landfill sites for waste uses land that could be put to more productive purposes.

Green buildings are not only concerned with energy and waste minimalization – they offer flexible robust investments able to cater for future change. It strikes me that many recent green buildings with their shallow floorplates, natural ventilation and simple use of daylight offer greater long-term flexibility than the over-complex, deep-plan, environmentally-sealed buildings of the past. The air-conditioned office or university building serves one purpose only and as society changes (and work patterns are currently undergoing radical restructuring) these buildings will become obsolete. We need buildings that can change within themselves and that can accommodate different functions over time.

The ten case studies in this book show that green buildings do not have to cost more, that they save money in terms of energy bills, and that by being environmentally friendly they lead to improvements in worker productivity through less absenteeism and greater company commitment. They are also, I believe, more attractive to look at than many earlier office and university buildings. Government has a role in encouraging better design through regulation, example and by funding energy advice schemes.

Regulation is of value up to a point. Our recent changes to Part L of the Building Regulations place a duty on designers and developers to raise insulation levels in order to help to conserve energy. But these are minimum standards and I am pleased to see that increasingly the industry is specifying far higher levels of insulation in the expectation that consumers expect more than the minimum.

Government, too, has begun to set an example through the buildings it constructs. Recent buildings for my department have incorporated best practice principles. The government has also made the commitment to subject all new and refurbished buildings for its own use to the Building Research Establishment Environmental Assessment Method (BREEAM). It seems to me that we cannot expect the private sector to follow green practices if government does not set an example. Even in Central London where air-conditioning is the norm, my department's new buildings have broken the mould by using chilled ceilings, displacement ventilation, combined heat and power plant, and building energy management systems.

Government also has a role in funding advice schemes which offer energy guidelines, publicize best practice, and undertake monitoring of the performance of green buildings. Both the BREEAM assessment, one of the earliest environmental labelling schemes adopted by any country in the world, and the Department of Trade and Industry's (DTI) Energy Design Advice Scheme, provide a powerful incentive for developers, designers and occupiers to move towards sustainable development. The BREEAM scheme, currently being emulated in Canada and Hong Kong, is an increasingly important element of the UK's drive to meet international obligations on CO_2 emissions. The government is on course to exceed its target to bring CO_2 emissions down to 1990 levels by the year 2000.

The construction industry is among our most cautious. I would like to see the benefits of green buildings more widely recognized. There are few more pressing challenges for government than to attain sustainable development while meeting the challenges ahead for economic growth. I have little doubt that green buildings do pay in financial, social and environmental terms. I hope that this book, and the two conferences upon which it is based, will help to promote the benefits of green design.

PART 1

The greening of the property industry

Chapter 1

Brian Edwards
University of
Huddersfield

1.1 a, b *Barclaycard
Headquarters, Northampton.
Architects: Fitzroy Robinson
and Partners.*

How do green buildings pay?

Most green buildings pay when measured by strictly financial criteria in that the extra construction costs of sustainable design are retrieved through reduced running costs in the first eight to ten years. In some particularly well-designed buildings there may be no additional building cost, as in the Leeds City Park (Chapter 10), or the saving in energy bills may pay for the green measures in less than five years, as in the Queen's Building at Anglia Polytechnic University (Chapter 12). Poor green design is where the additional construction costs are never recovered through reduced heating, lighting or ventilation bills, or increased productivity as a result of higher comfort levels.

To be effective commercially, socially and environmentally, sustainable design needs to give measurable benefits. It is not sufficient, especially in the rigorous field of commercial or educational buildings, to view green design as an act of faith or Utopianism. To persuade private developers and clients in the public sector to risk new approaches and use new sustainable technologies there needs to be maximum benefit and minimum financial exposure.

Direct benefits

The principal benefits of green design for the developers are:

- economies in fuel bills (either for owner or tenant)
- market advantage;
- lower long-term exposure to environmental or health problems;
- greater productivity of workforce.

The risks are:

- will the building perform as predicted?
- are the 'green' costs affordable?
- is the technology reliable?

a

Glazed roof heats air
to promote stack effect

Rainwater collected
for artificial lake

Direct and reflected
light enters offices
from the atrium

Deep reveals and *brise
soleil* provide shading
for south elevation

15m deep offices allow
natural ventilation and
maximum daylight

High thermal performance
to perimeter walls
and windows

Light shelves provide
indirect daylighting
for offices

Openable windows

Lake supplies chillers
and water sprinklers

Landscaping modifies
air cooling in summer and
air warming in winter

Chilled water (15-16 °C) from lake supplies chilled beams

b

1.2 *Full life-cycle assessment supports green architecture, as here at the Broadgate development, London. Architects: Arup Associates and Skidmore Owings and Merril.*

1.3 *Student residences heated by solar power at Strathclyde University. Architects: GRM Kennedy and Partners with Kaiser Bautechnik.*

These advantages and disadvantages apply whether the developer is in the private or public sector.

An example of a successful green building is the headquarters of the NMB in Amsterdam constructed in 1990. Lord Rodgers, in his presentation to the conference 'Green Buildings Pay' in 1996, reported that the NMB building saved more than £300 000 a year in energy costs against a conventional office building of similar size. The energy consumption is one-twelfth that of the bank's former building allowing the owner to calculate that the additional cost of plant and equipment was paid for in three months of occupation. In addition, NMB have found that absenteeism is 15% lower than in the old building adding considerably to the bank's performance. Here the bank, built to low-energy and high environmental standards, with plenty of user control over the temperature and humidity of working areas, has proved a success in financial and productivity terms.

The construction of office buildings to attract future tenants is not unlike the building of university accommodation to attract students. In both cases green design is about keeping running costs down, providing a healthy and attractive building, and projecting an image through architecture that has market appeal. Increasingly office workers and students expect a working environment which is responsive to their needs at a personal level by giving them control over their workspace,

while also expressing in the values of the building a concern for wider global problems.

The typical office in the UK consumes $200kWh/m^2$ over a typical year. Best practice aims to reduce this to $100kWh/m^2$ and several examples in this book achieve even better figures. The Environmental Building recently completed at the Building Research Establishment's (BRE) headquarters near Watford (Chapter 11) is expected to achieve an energy rating of $80kWh/m^2$, which is close to the best practice in the USA and Canada where $75kWh/m^2$ has been recorded.[1] In these countries greater use of photovoltaics and higher levels of construction achieve by engineering means what in the UK is sought by natural ventilation and more low-technology building methods. However, whether high or low-tech approaches are adopted the target of $100kWh/m^2$ is increasingly the bench mark for good design.

The main benefits of green design to a developer are financial: taking a long-term view, the running costs will pay several times over for the greater initial investment. In many cases the distinctive form of a building designed to sustainable principles will set the building apart for neighbours and provide a cachet that attracts tenants. Just as some cars and washing machines are sold as being green (or greener than competitors) so, too, green buildings will appeal to a section of the

1.4 a, b *Commerzbank Headquarters, Frankfurt. Architects: Foster and Partners.*

a

b

—   are healthier to use;

—   have psychological advantage;

—   enhance company image.

Healthier to use

The use of more natural sources of light, solar energy for heating or cooling, and more organic materials in construction all add up to a healthier building than that represented by the typical air-conditioned office or university building. Healthy buildings which seek to work with climate and use natural materials in construction and finishes tend to suffer from lower levels of sickness and absenteeism. This has obvious advantages in terms of continuity of work and productivity which reflects upon company balance sheets. Taking university accommodation, healthy, low-energy buildings will (as our case studies show) result in contented students, the attraction of good quality academic staff, and improved output all round.

Psychological advantage

People feel 'better' in green buildings. They are not only healthier, but they claim an enhanced sense of wellbeing. The ability to open windows, to activate their own blinds, to pass through

property market. To have comprehensive application, green buildings need to show they pay in less direct ways.

Indirect benefits

There are three ways in which sustainable design benefits both the developers and their tenants and has an indirect bearing upon balance sheets. Green buildings:

1.5 *Cable and Wireless College, Coventry, sets an admirable example of attractive green design. Architects: MacCormac Jamieson Prichard.*

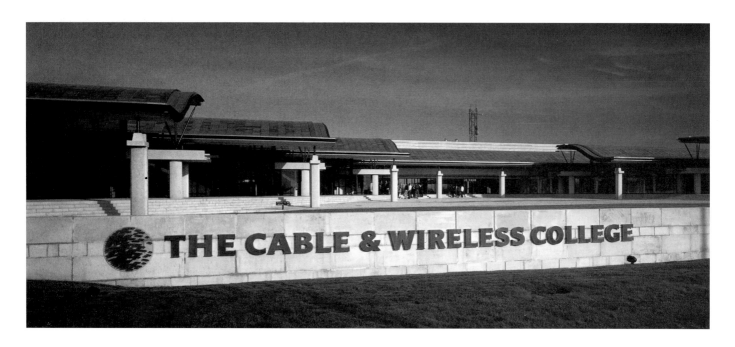

well-planted atria or winter gardens, to have trees and planting immediately outside their windows, and to smell the breeze, all lead to a sense of feeling better about work, thereby increasing productivity. In the USA, research has shown that the 'feel good factor' of green design has improved workplace performance sufficient to pay for a typical building's annual energy bills. A 1% reduction in absenteeism pays for the energy costs of a typical commercial building. The 'feel good factor' also leads to greater tolerance of temperature variations. The psychological dimension recognized increasingly by facilities managers has begun to influence building briefs.

Enhance company image

Green design is normally the result of holistic thinking by a team of professionals, including the client, who share similar environmental ideals. To be effective green design needs to consider many factors from the new financial equations implicit in sustainability to the likely reactions of workers and clients. The design team juggles with capital and running costs on the one hand, and balances between energy use, environmental impact and ecology on the other. Only an open, flexible view of design allows this to happen, and the resulting building embodying green principles will inevitably influence the company that uses it. As a consequence the building leads to subtle changes in the culture of the company and the outlook of the workers. Although a developer or public client may specify a low-energy building, the consequences may be more profound than a mere saving in annual fuel bills.

The Body Shop's green outlook, for instance, influences its products, process and building procurement, and in turn has an impact upon the people who both work for and supply the company, or are sub-contracted by it. The same is true of Cable and Wireless (Chapter 14), which links building procurement to the company's environmental policy, setting an example to others and also saving money. The holistic outlook can spread from a company to its buildings, the building to the company, and the company to the individual, thereby enhancing its image.

Wider global benefits

The term 'green buildings pay' has so far been seen in the context of financial benefits – both direct and indirect – to those who undertake building development. There are several other ways in which sustainable design pays, although the currency here is not so much financial as global. Buildings are a major consumer of fossil fuels and other resources. The Brundtland

1.6 *Inland Revenue Building, Nottingham, sets a good example of low-energy design. Architects: Michael Hopkins and Partners.*

Commission's definition of sustainability (1987) is development that 'meets the needs of the present without compromising the ability of future generations to meet their needs'. In the UK buildings account for about 50% of all energy use (contributing about the same amount to climate damaging CO_2 production), their construction uses nearly 50% of all raw materials used by industry, they consume 40% of the UK's water, and they are the major of imported hardwoods – most of which have their origins in distant rainforests.

The philosophy of green buildings is not only a question of designing for low-energy use, but of considering in an integrated way the whole range of environmental and ecological impacts involved. In order to consider in a systematic fashion the broader benefits of green design each building should be evaluated against the following perspectives:

- global warming;
- ozone layer depletion;
- biodiversity;
- product miles;
- recycling.

Global warming

What are the impacts upon global climate instability in terms of CO_2 production? Are the most energy-efficient means being adopted to heat, light and ventilate the building? Are renewable sources of energy being exploited, at least for part of the time? Is waste heat being recovered or lost to the atmosphere?

CO_2 is, of course, involved in both the running and construction of the building. What are the energy costs of construction (the energy needed to make a brick will drive a family car for eight to ten miles), and what is the payback period in energy terms of using high embodied energy materials such as aluminium or steel?

The global warming equation is complex but vital since climate change is likely to be the greatest destabilising force politically and socially of the next century. Buildings that greatly reduce their CO_2 production, use materials such as home-grown softwoods (which beneficially balance the CO_2 equation), and are designed as part of self-sufficient carbon communities where buildings and forests exchange oxygen for CO_2, all point the way forward. These projects act as exemplars influencing practice in Britain and further afield.

Ozone layer depletion

Although the thinning of the ozone layer and global warming share certain similarities, the problems are quite distinct. However, a building which is low-energy in design is likely also to add little to the thinning of the ozone layer. About a half of ozone damage is caused by chlorofluorocarbons (CFCs) used in connection with air-conditioned, usually high-energy buildings. Designing with natural ventilation avoids ozone damage which has led to 60 000 extra cases of skin cancer a year in the UK alone because of the additional ultra-violet light.

Although the Montreal Protocol (1990) and subsequent European Union directives have begun to phase out the production of CFCs they remain in use in many commercial and educational buildings. Air-conditioning, a requirement for many commercial developments in city-centre locations, tends not to be favoured by building occupiers. A survey by Richard Ellis & Company showed that 89% of tenants preferred non-air-conditioned offices. Its specification by a cautious property industry, however, is still the norm since it allows for all levels of tenant need. Undermining the practice of air-conditioning through alternative approaches to office design, which appeal to user comfort rather than commercial perceptions, will in time phase out the need for CFCs. With hindsight, over-

.7 *Typical office buildings of
the 1980s were big users of
CFCs as well as fossil fuels*

specification of offices in the 1980s was one of the reasons for the collapse of the property market.

Biodiversity

The need to maintain global biodiversity was, like the earlier two points, part of the agreement entered into by the UK and many other world governments at the Rio Summit in 1992. Buildings influence biodiversity in many ways – they are home to species other than man, and the choice of materials used in their construction affects the destruction of endangered global habitats and the creation of others. The specification of hardwoods (many different species are used in commercial buildings) has an impact upon forests at home and abroad. For example, to specify beech helps to conserve domestic and European forests, but to use teak or mahogany threatens more distant rainforests which are not usually managed on sustainable lines.

Biodiversity is also influenced by the choice of more everyday materials such as concrete or brick. The extraction of aggregates, clay, chalk and limestone all alter the face of the land creating gravel pits and quarries that can either be left as wildlife areas or used for landfill sites. In either case, valuable land is lost to agriculture and adds to our growing bank of degraded landscapes (about 12% of the land area of Britain).

Since buildings are colonized by many species other than man they can inadvertently provide shelter for locally endangered species such as bats, or become havens for less desirable colonizers such as cockroaches. Green buildings use organic materials and have a natural process that tends to be more inviting than more sterile building environments. Effective building maintenance is required to ensure that the benign conditions created for man are not unduly exploited by insect colonies, pigeons or roosting starlings. The solar protection screens provided at the edge of many office buildings, for example, provide ready perches for the city's wildlife. The answer increasingly adopted in urban areas is to have an outer glazed protective wall up to two metres forward of the building envelope with solar screens and daylight shelves in the airspace.

Product miles

The environmental footprint of a building can be very extensive. One way to measure this is to use the concept of 'product miles' where the product weight, distance and means of transport are considered. Building materials which are imported from other countries involve energy use in transportation,

1.8 *The Mistral Building,
Reading, uses European timber
from sustainable forests.
Architects: Foster and Partners.*

disturbance over long distances if carried by road or air, and leave a trail of pollution across continents. As a general rule it is better to use local products, especially bulky ones, if the environmental impacts are to be minimized.

The environmental impact equation is complex if all the ramifications are followed through. To obtain high-energy performance softwood windows the architect often has to specify suppliers in Sweden, compost toilets are manufactured in Canada, boilers that use waste products (such as domestic or textile refuse) are made in Denmark. Green products may not be available locally, certainly not to the standard demanded of commercial, government or university developers.

Recycling

As the earth becomes more crowded and the standard of living rises, resources will increasingly be in short supply. Though fossil fuels are now abundant they will in time become scarce and expensive – most probably within the lifespan of most buildings now being designed. The same is true of plastics, steel, aluminium and clay products, etc. The long-term answer is to design buildings that:

— in corporate the maximum possible amount of recycled

material (either directly or indirectly);
— allow for ready dismantling and reuse.

Several of the case studies in this book incorporate recycled materials and some are designed so that the building itself can be readily recycled, either through functional change or the re-employment of elements of construction.

Buildings are reservoirs of resource investment which are carried across generations. In most buildings the investment in energy and materials has been made wisely, in others there is the need for upgrading. This is particularly true of those constructed in the 1960s when low specification levels and plentiful supplies of energy led to a decade of leaky, poor-performance buildings. Generally buildings are, unlike most consumer goods such as cars, long-term asset resources. The implications are two-fold: first, only rarely should buildings be demolished, but they should be adapted periodically, especially to new energy technologies. Second, buildings should seek to use recycled components, or materials from other industries. An example is the Groundwork Trust headquarters building in Jarrow, near Newcastle, which uses creeper-clad external solar protection made from redundant trawler nets held in place by scrap Ford Transit clutch housings.

Integrating energy, environmental and ecological perspectives

Buildings of the future will increasingly incorporate environmental, ecological and energy factors into the design at a conceptual level. Green design is not a matter of addressing the environmental problems society faces as a bolt-on addition to existing practice, but of evolving design from the starting point of these three perspectives. This, of course, requires a client sympathetic to these ideals, users who understand and value the concepts, and designers and contractors who as a team evolve the design with a green outlook.

Within the triangle formed by Energy, Environment and Ecology, green design can take its precise position depending upon local circumstance.

Where energy costs are the main determining factor, the resultant building will be different from one in which ecology is the prominent force, likewise an urban building will be different from a rural one. However, in each case 'green building will

1.9 *Buildings constructed from components and panels, such as the Kabuki-cho Building, Tokyo, are more readily dismantled than monolithic ones, allowing for potential recycling. Architects: Richard Rogers Partnership.*

1.10 *Central atrium and solar chimney, Groundwork Trust Office, Jarrow, near Newcastle. Architect: Carol Townsend of EarthSense.*

pay' by either saving the client money or by helping to save the planet. In reducing developer and tenant costs through responsible green design, the client is helping to conserve world resources of fossil fuels, and in burning less is easing the problems of climate change.

The way to solve the environmental problem is by legislation, education and example. Legislation is important since it gives legitimacy to new directions – the law provides fresh parameters and identifies new frontiers for action. Education is equally crucial: it establishes the climate of opinion through debate and criticism for action. Such criticism is founded on the example of precedent, which properly monitored provides the bench mark for the future. The examples in this book and the

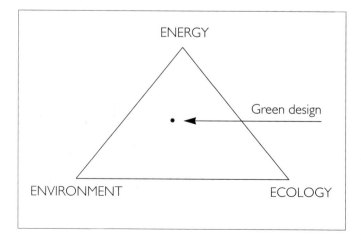

1.11 *Facade design at Marston Book Building, Milton Park, Oxfordshire, exploits natural ventilation and simple solar screening. Architects: David Lloyd Jones (with RMJM).*

1.12 *Design sketch for British Gas offices, Leeds City Office Park. Architects: Peter Foggo Associates.*

Table 1.1 Annual performance targets for energy-efficient offices

Component load	Narrow-plan building Gas and electric (kWh/m²)	Narrow-plan building All electric (kWh/m²)	Deep-plan building Gas and electric (kWh/m²)	Deep-plan building All electric (kWh/m²)
Lighting	10	10	15	15
Fans and pumps	6	3	8	5
Small power	20	20	20	20
Space heating	40	30	40	30
Domestic hot water supply	7	5	7	5
Total electricity	36	68	43	75
Total gas	47	–	47	–
Carbon dioxide emissions (kg/m²)	34	47	39	52

Source: *A Performance Specification for the Energy Efficient Office of the Future*, Department of the Environment, Energy Efficiency Office, December 1995, p. 6.

perspectives of those in the property industry provide pathways for a more sustainable future. They are not perfect, but they face in the right direction. Taken together environmental laws (and here CO_2 taxes may play a positive role in the future), environmental education in the property and construction industry, and the tangible example of built projects will collectively achieve the consensus that green buildings do pay.

Briefing for sustainable design

The role of the brief is crucial if sustainable design is to become commonplace. One reason why so many office and educational buildings perform badly from an environmental point of view is overspecification. Air-conditioning is specified in the brief yet users do not want it. High-technology air-sealed facades are employed where natural ventilation is the better option and deep-plan buildings are designed where shallow plan provides greater flexibility and user comfort. To combat this problem the Energy Efficiency Office at the Department of the Environment (DoE) has issued the following guiding principles for the energy-efficient office:

- reduce energy loads wherever possible;
- provide energy input as efficiently as possible;
- minimize plant operation times – default to 'off' or 'standby';
- use the simplest solutions that will satisfy the client's requirements and can be managed by the end user.

The principles need to address key areas of performance from the design of lighting (especially the effective use of daylight and controls on artificial lighting), visual comfort, psychological well-being, health and passive control of the working environment.

These guiding principles translate into briefing points, which help in achieving an energy and environmentally friendly office or workplace of the future.[2] Points to consider are:

- detailed user needs;
- selection of appropriate technologies;
- use of innovative (and tested) design ideas;
- maximum passive environmental control;
- minimum use of complex HVAC services;
- energy efficiency considered at all stages;

- optimization of comfort and health standards;
- buildability and replaceability;
- on-site/modular/pre-fab construction opportunities;
- environmental and ecological impact of building;
- future flexibility;
- commissioning appropriate level of specification;
- training of building occupiers in operation of environmental systems.

Clearly not all building designs need to address each point, but the briefing checklist allows the right mix of parameters to be established. It is also evident that buildings in contaminated or polluted urban areas will have different sustainable characteristics from those on the city edge or greenfield sites. The parameters also point towards the narrow-plan, naturally ventilated and daylit office of the future (perhaps with alternate atria and open light wells). Although the checklist embraces energy, environmental and ecology issues, it is generally true that a building of low-energy consumption (capital and revenue energy costs) is also likely to have reduced impacts elsewhere.

Table 1.2 Sustainability indicators for buildings

- move from fossil fuel to renewable energy sources
- efficient use of other resources
- waste minimization
- closing cycles
- life-cycle assessment
- pollution
- environmental capacity
- biodiversity
- land-use diversity
- health, safety and security
- access for all
- non-car access
- local sourcing
- durability
- flexibility
- social equity
- local distinctiveness/richness driven by environmental factors

1.13 *BREEAM logo.*

Environmental quality standards: the example of the Building Research Establishment Environmental Assessment Method (BREEAM)

Once the brief has been prepared the architect and engineer can begin to design the building with green perspectives in mind. It is often advantageous to test the evolving design against bench marks of good practice. One of the best known is BREEAM, developed by the Building Research Establishment (BRE) to provide developers with an independent assessment of the overall environmental credentials of the building. The scheme is comprehensive, tested and monitored by evaluation of buildings in use, and covers a range of building types including offices. Buildings are given a rating on a scale of Fair, Good, Very Good and Excellent. About 25% of all new offices in the UK has been subject to a BREEAM assessment since 1991.

BREEAM is comprehensive, dealing not only with energy performance but issues ranging from global atmospheric pollution to the impact of the building upon the local environment. It also embraces the comfort and health of building users. The main factors measured or assessed are:

- carbon-dioxide emissions with quantified bench marks;
- healthy building features;
- air quality and ventilation;
- minimization of ozone depletion and acid rain;
- recycling and reuse of materials;
- ecology of the site;
- water conservation;
- noise;
- risk of legionnaire's disease;
- hazardous materials;
- lighting.[3]

BREEAM allows a building's likely performance to be predicted, benefiting the designer as well as client. An early assessment allows alternative options to be explored before ideas have hardened. With construction in the UK consuming 366 million tonnes of materials per year,[4] building design has profound implications for environmental management generally.

The environmental quality standard represented by BREEAM encourages the development community to take a stake in environmental matters. The wide parameters of the assessment give weight to legitimate user needs, such as health and comfort. The assessment also provides investors with independent reassurance over any risks involved in new environmental technologies, and it allows government to measure performance against policy objectives. Although energy has been the main thrust of BREEAM to date, new concerns such as water shortage, fit well into the matrix of environmental criteria adopted.

BREEAM provides the following benefits for the construction industry:

- developers can improve sales by promoting the high environmental performance of their buildings;
- designers can demonstrate the environmental achievements of their work;
- landlords can audit the property from an environmental point of view;
- managers can reassure employees that the working environment is healthy and of high quality.[5]

These lead to improved productivity, enhanced value, greater profit, and to development which has reduced adverse impact upon the environment. In this sense green building does pay.

1.14 *Stockley Park sets a new bench mark for low-energy, high environmental design. Masterplan: Arup Associates.*

The BREEAM audit has recently been extended from the realm of office design to office occupation. The BRE Toolkit allows the environmental impact of office-based businesses to be evaluated. It is no good if the architect creates energy efficient workspace only for the company occupying the office not to use good environmental practices. Toolkit allows the relationship between capital and running costs to be understood, not just with regard to energy but to wider environmental impacts. Designed primarily for facilities or office managers, Toolkit is a self-assessment which helps to improve environmental performance and save money. Like BREEAM, it is concerned with direct impacts such as energy, water, paper use and waste management, and indirect ones such as commuting, business travel and internal air quality.[6] There are 17 sections that provide a comprehensive environmental assessment of the office in occupation.

Energy Design Advice Service (EDAS)

Another useful tool in assessing the likely energy performance of a building at the design stage is EDAS, an independent energy auditing scheme sponsored by the Department of Trade and Industry (DTI). The EDAS consultation is concerned primarily with energy performance. In particular it provides a

Warm stratified air exhausts to outside via wind tower.

Prevailing wind assists exhaust air through wind tower.

Warm stratified air exhausts via atrium.

External shading and light shelves on south elevations block direct sunlight

Fresh air intake from cool, shaded courtyards.

Fan assisted ventilation flues supply air.

Summer Operation

detailed prediction of expected energy loads per square metre and likely savings in the volume of carbon dioxide (CO_2) emitted. Also, since EDAS can provide several consultations during the different stages of the design process, it offers a finer level of energy modelling than under BREEAM's broad-brush approach.

The effect of BREEAM and EDAS has begun to change perceptions in the development industry and design professions. Employing energy-conscious design techniques does not have to cost more (though often it does). Modelling environmental and energy impacts at the design stage allows the relationship between capital and running costs to be understood with greater clarity than in the past. Evidence from monitoring the performance of buildings constructed to higher energy standards (the PowerGen Building, Coventry, Chapter 8, is an example) indicate that good green design is no more expensive than conventional practice. As a new generation of environmentally friendly buildings is constructed, it is increasingly clear that such buildings have the potential to save money by reducing energy costs but without significant increase in capital costs.

Energy labelling

The overwhelming need to use energy more efficiently and to replace fossil fuels by renewables in order to help to stabilize CO_2 emissions[7] has given greater urgency to the role of the advice schemes outlined and to tightening legislative standards. It is clear from the case studies that cost is less of an impediment to progress than ignorance. The UK government in 1996 introduced compulsory energy labelling for new housing under Part L of the Building Regulations and in 1997 engaged in consulting the property industry over a similar scheme for non-domestic buildings.

Energy labelling has two main benefits: it allows tenants and building owners to know in advance what the fuel bills are likely to be; and in drawing attention to energy costs, encourages the generation of low-energy buildings. Energy labelling will raise the general awareness of energy efficiency among designers and developers alike.

Many measures outlined in this book do not add to costs. Good practice such as the correct building orientation and window size, and the use of natural ventilation adds nothing to

Top: Lycée Albert Camus, Fréjus, France.
Architects: Foster and Partners.

Bottom: Commerzbank Headquarters,
Frankfurt. Architects: Foster and Partners.

Top: Mistral Building, Reading.
Architects: Foster and Partners.

Bottom: EDF Headquarters, Bordeaux.
Architects: Foster and Partners.

Right: Helicon Building, London:
Architects: Sheppard Robson.

Left: Elizabeth Fry Building, University of East Anglia.
Architects: John Miller and Partners.

Below (both pictures):
PowerGen Building, Coventry.
Architects: Bennetts Associates.

Below and right: The Environmental Building at the Building Research Establishment (BRE), Garston. Architects: Feilden Clegg.

Bottom: Cable and Wireless College, Coventry. Architects: MacCormac Jamieson Prichard.

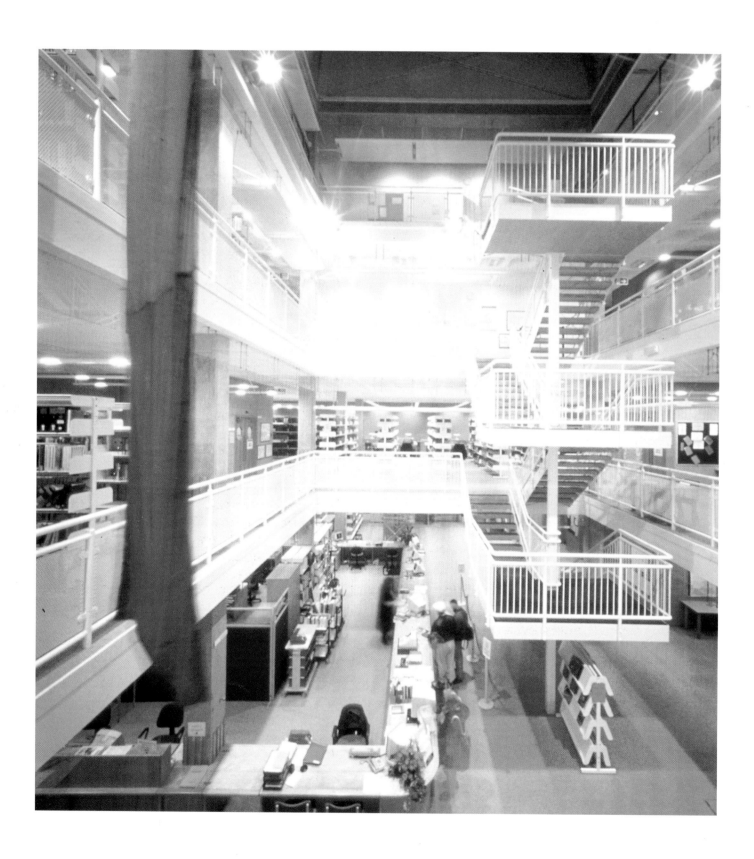

Atrium, Anglia Polytechnic University. Architects:
ECD Architects.

capital cost yet will save thousands of pounds per year in energy bills; while saving the capital costs of air-conditioning leads to a significant reduction in the volume of CO_2 emitted.

The question posed earlier about whether green buildings do pay has both financial and moral dimensions. There is growing evidence from built projects than in monetary terms alone green buildings do represent a sounder long-term investment than more conventionally designed buildings. But while financial arguments are important, there is also the need to consider the health, comfort and wellbeing of the building occupants and the planet at large.

As sustainability gains greater moral urgency so, too, building development is increasingly responding to many pressing environmental issues rather than just a single one. Returning to the example of the new Groundwork Trust offices at Jarrow, this building incorporates evaporative cooling from a fountain in the triangular atrium; creepers and deciduous trees provide solar shading; solar energy and wind power are both exploited; and underfloor heating uses groundwater and a heat pump. The design by architect Carol Townsend embraces many environmental issues in a holistic fashion. The anticipated energy load is expected to be 75kWh/sq m/year as against the norm for cellular, naturally ventilated offices of 250kWh/sq m/year, and 400–600kWh/sq m/year for air conditioned offices.[8] Such significant and measurable advantages auger well for a new generation of leaner office buildings.

Summary of principles

The six guiding principles found in the green design are:

- environmental design appropriate to context;
- use of simple, robust techniques rather than unnecessary complexity;
- exploitation of thermal capacity of structure;
- exploitation of natural ventilation as the prime means of cooling;
- use of easily understood building controls;
- avoidance of over-sized plant with upgradability provided at design stage.[9]

The case studies illustrate these and other principles of green design. The main benefits perceived by developers and users of green buildings are:

- low cost in use (in energy and maintenance terms);
- higher environmental quality of workplace leading to happier, healthier, more productive staff;
- higher occupant control over internal environment;
- lower built-in obsolescence of services;
- enhanced company and building image.[10]

References

1. David Olivier, *Energy Efficiency and Renewables: Recent North American Experience*, 1996, p. viii.
2. *A Performance Specification for the Energy Efficient Office of the Future* (Report 30), Department of the Environment, Energy Efficiency Best Practice Programme, December 1995, p. 3.
3. Dave Hampton, 'Environmental Issues', *Energy World*, May 1996, p. 9.
4. *BREEAM: An Introduction* (leaflet), Building Research Establishment, no date.
5. Ibid, this list is an abbreviation.
6. *The Office Toolkit*, leaflet, BRE, 1996.
7. *EDAS Communique*, Issue 5, 1996.
8. *EDAS Case Study N008*, 'Eco Offices', Jarrow, Tyneside, UK.
9. Adapted from Bill Bordass, 'Avoiding office air-conditioning', *The Architects' Journal*, 20 July 1995, pp. 37–39.
10. 'Green Buildings: Benefits and Barriers', *Building Services*, April 1996, pp. 40-41.

Chapter 2

William McKee,
Director General,
British Property
Federation

Green buildings and the UK property industry

Green office buildings will become commonplace only if they take account of the principles and philosophy of the commercial property industry. Sustainable development is unlikely to materialize if it ignores the economic constraints under which the industry operates. In particular, the decision to provide new commercial buildings is judged against their performance as an asset and their ability to attract tenants thereby generating good rental levels and ultimately, adequate yields.

The property industry has changed substantially since the 1980s. With low inflation, office building returns will depend largely on active management, including a measurable improvement in quality. This is where green buildings may well offer advantages over non-sustainable competitors; there is growing evidence that the healthy, naturally lit and ventilated modern office is seen by occupiers as a genuine improvement.

New tenant needs

The property market in the UK has undergone significant and probably irreversible change over the past five years. Changing business practices have led to downsizing of companies, outsourcing of many tasks, hot-desking (where desks are shared rather than owned), and greater globalization. The result is that tenant companies strive for the minimum building occupational costs conducive to effective operation. Here green buildings can have a perceived edge – they are seen as costing less to run in energy terms while providing healthy workspace where staff are likely to be contented and hence more productive. In this sense providing a wholesome working environment is seen as good business, and the basis of a sound investment by the property industry.

As the market has undergone these threshold changes, buildings are seen less as a potential asset growth and more as

2.1 *Ionica Building, Cambridge.*
Architects: RH Partnership.

a factor of production. At the same time, real estate has become a boardroom issue and buildings another company outgoing which should be properly measured and evaluated, not just rental levels. The issues which matter to the company facilities manager are flexibility, health and safety, running costs, effects upon absenteeism, tenant perception, etc. In the 1980s the property industry determined specification levels, size and quality of accommodation, but the emphasis is shifting to the customer. Tenants now influence building design to a far greater degree and it is tenant power which is leading the incorporation of green principles into the commercial property market.

As companies have downsized and decentralized, the demand for different kinds and size of office space has

intensified. For example, the headquarters building has shrunk in size, and to a degree also, in visible ostentation. The demand for large, environmentally sealed office building of 100 000ft^2 (10 000m^2) is reducing and even large government departments in Central London prefer smaller units. Within the shorter business-plan horizons of today's typical office tenants, the accommodation element has to meet stricter standards of performance and flexibility than in the past. Tenants are aware of sick building syndrome, conscious of the hidden costs of poorly designed buildings, and frequently strive to incorporate good environmental practice into their operations (such as the use of recycled paper and low-energy light bulbs). These new tenant needs, particularly whole life costing, are leading to a change in outlook from the property industry. For example

2.2 *Finsbury Avenue,*
Broadgate. Architects:
Arup Associates.

with 89% of office occupiers against air-conditioned buildings (according to a survey carried out by Richard Ellis and Partners in 1992), tenant power is fast altering the commercial property industry.

Consequently as tenant need changes under new company priorities, the low-specification office buildings of the 1960s or the over-specified deep-plan offices of the 1980s, also need to change. Adapting and upgrading the present stock to meet these new tenant needs and fresh environmental standards represents an investment as important as in new office construction. Although much of this upgrading is to meet new business standards demanded by some of the emerging companies of the 1990s, it offers the opportunity to introduce new green measures. Besides green initiatives there are other

Table 2.1 Critical parameters for the Green Office

Plan depth	13.5–15m (for draught-free cross-ventilation)
Window to core	6–12m
Planning grid	1.5m
Column grid	6m, 7.5m or 9m
Floor to ceiling height	2600–2750mm
Raised floor zone	150mm
Suspended ceiling zone	150mm

Source: *Best Practice in the Specification for Offices*, British Council for Offices, 1997.

Table 2.2 Critical criteria for the green office

- occupational density: 1 person per 14m² net
- integrate active systems of indoor climate control (building services) with passive systems (building fabric)
- orientate building to reduce glare and unwanted solar heat whilst maximizing daylight
- exploit potential of building facade in order to provide solar shading
- exploit atria and malls (glazed streets) for stack effect and cross-ventilation
- use natural ventilation in office areas and air-conditioning in 'hot spots'
- exploit thermal capacity of building fabric for day and night-time cooling
- adopt a greater internal temperature range

Source: *Best Practice in the Specification for Offices*, British Council for Offices, 1997.

changes to the structure of the property industry. Location matters more than in the past and a good external environment and access to reliable public transport is seen as increasingly important by government.

The running costs of a green building

The demise of the 'trophy' building has corresponded to the emergence of more homogeneous yardsticks of performance. Offices are more likely these days to be built to standard depths of floorplate (determined by daylight penetration) and more formulaic units of accommodation. A reduction in bespoke specification levels has helped to reduce the cost of providing office space. Compared to a decade ago, the real cost of office occupation has fallen, partly as a result of low-energy costs due to better design. Also, changing relationships between owner and tenant (the result of the demand for more flexible leases) has resulted in contracts where the building owner (not tenant) pays the energy bills. This has focused owners' attention on running costs, adding to the drive to save unnecessary energy consumption and increasing interest by the property industry in low-energy design.

There are, however, serious constraints on the ability of the British property industry to deliver green buildings on a large scale. It is increasingly difficult to meet sustainable design objectives when the economic climate is unfavourable. There is also a lack of research on the performance of green buildings. The development industry needs hard information on the relative energy efficiency of different types of green offices, as well as the views of tenants and individual office workers.

Although it is now commonly stated that green buildings lead to more productive working, less absenteeism and a greater commitment from the office worker to the company, there is little systematic evidence available to confirm the claim. In America research has shown that green offices lead to at least a 1% improvement in productivity, but information for the UK is not available. Little is known also of the asset performance of green commercial buildings.

As environmental standards rise one should assume that buildings designed in a green fashion will retain their value better than competitors, but as yet the industry has no hard figures to confirm or deny this. Since some low-energy buildings are excessively complex in operation, green design may, in fact, bring about speedier obsolescence and reduced value over time. Certainly for the property industry sustainability needs to lead to a generation of simple, readily understood offices.

Generally speaking, green buildings tend to cost more to construct than conventional offices. The industry would normally expect the extra cost of initiatives such as low-energy design and the use of natural non-toxic materials to be recovered in five to eight years. Beyond that the risks are too high in the uncertain business of property development. There are many green opportunities to be taken in the property industry, but sustainable development must be wedded to commercial reality and viability.

There is no doubt that the British property industry (i.e. property companies, institutions and pension funds) is generally supportive of the drive towards environmentally designed buildings, but the difficulties should not be underestimated. The key to more green offices lies not so much in developing the technical side but in adjusting the economic arguments in favour of more sustainable solutions. The technology of green buildings is well understood and the benefits widely acknowledged, but in the current market circumstances where there is an over-supply of commercial floor space it is difficult to see the economic return in adapting present offices in a green fashion. The comparatively low rate of new development is such that genuine improvement lies in tackling the existing stock to

2.3 *London's Broadgate develop-*
ment combines green design with
good access to public transport.
Architects: Arup Associates and
Skidmore Owings and Merrill.

2.4 *Simple solar screening with planting adds to the success of the Broadgate Development. Architects: Arup Associates and Skidmore Owings and Merrill.*

make it more energy efficient, healthier to use, and more responsive to individual need. Unfortunately green rehabilitation is less well understood than green design. Adapting buildings constructed over the past 30 years from a green perspective is fraught with difficulties. Many have fairly low floor-to-ceiling heights, the structural arrangements offer little flexibility, sites are often polluted or noisy, and deep floor plans are commonplace.

Conclusion

Clients will innovate in green technologies, but only if they are tried and tested. The office building is not the place to test out new design approaches or to experiment with emerging sustainable technologies. The margins in the property industry cannot carry that degree of risk. The property industry should not be seen by government, research councils, designers and engineers as a laboratory for developing and testing new office prototypes. For example, low-energy systems in buildings do not work all the time. With natural approaches (such as stack effect ventilation, solar flueing, even natural lighting) the building needs to provide mechanical back-up. Having two systems installed can be expensive, adds to operational complexity, and can affect the value of the property even if it saves money in

Table 2.3 Advantages of energy-efficient builds: Positive benefits from specifying energy efficient buildings:

— they need not cost more;

— they have lower running costs;

— they offer a more responsive environment to occupants;

— they justify additional rental value;

— they add to the sale value of the builings;

— They will be simpler to re-lease in the future;

— Energy efficiency is an enormous contributor to a sustainable resources policy;

— they have a marketing advantage because of their other energy related features;

— the most energy efficient building is one which provides the specified internal environment for the minimum energy cost.

Source: BRECSU, 1997

the short term. What the industry requires is added value through good green design; value measured in improved lettability and enhanced asset strength. Certain green approaches have been shown to decrease confidence and undermine property investment. The risks must be kept low by incorporating only simple green technologies and those which have been tried and tested elsewhere.

As mentioned earlier, green approaches to office building will have greater impact upon the perception of investors if they can be shown to offer improvements in returns. From the occupier's point of view, buildings which are environmentally friendly and offer a better place to work, have a market advantage over their rivals', and in the increasingly competitive world of building the health and wellbeing of office staff tends to be more important than relatively small decreases in energy bills. If green offices can deliver measurable benefits to productivity while also achieving say a 40% reduction in energy costs, then the industry will begin to experiment with new office layouts and new sustainable technologies. Without these tangible economic benefits the property industry will not be seduced by the sheer excitement of new green approaches to building engineering.

Chapter 3

Alan Rowe,
Lansdown Estates
Group

Market advantage through green design

The property company Lansdown Estates Group (a subsidiary of MEPC) has long had an interest in low-energy design. At Milton Park, a mixed-use business estate of 100 hectares near Abingdon, Oxfordshire, the company has been constructing green commercial buildings for a variety of occupiers since 1989. Using this experience, Lansdown Estates participated in the Department of Energy's Passive Solar Design research project providing case studies of good practice. In 1994 it also supported the Environmental Code of Practice for Buildings and their Services produced by the Building Services Research and Information Association (BSRIA).

The reason for this interest in green design is a combination of financial expediency, a concern for user comfort, an interest in wider environmental questions, long-term flexibility, and our perception of market advantage.

Financial expediency

The low level of demand for air-conditioned space, when combined with its high cost in relation to rental values in a business park location such as Milton Park (currently around £140/m^2 for new speculative naturally ventilated B1 office space and £70/m^2 for new speculative B8 space), will not usually support sealed mechanically ventilated office buildings. Capital costs, running costs and depreciation costs mean that Lansdown Estates look to eliminate the requirements for air-conditioning where possible. However, we do design our buildings so that they have an upgrade path and can adapt to full or partial air-conditioning should occupiers so require. This seems sensible in a period of transition.

User comfort

Lansdown Estates devotes significant time to maintaining close contact with existing occupiers at Milton Park through its site-

3.1 *Section, New Mill House, 183 Milton Park, Oxfordshire. Architects: RMJM.*

3.2 *Comparison of annual operating costs of property at Milton Park, Oxfordshire.*

SOUTH

NORTH

PREVAILING WIND

SUNBREAKERS

VENTILATION FOR NIGHT TIME COOLING AND TO PREVENT HEAT BUILD UP IN CEILING VOID

COURTYARD CREATES NEGATIVE PRESSURE

CL
2800
OFFICES

FFL
CL
1225

COLONNADE PROVIDES SOLAR PROTECTION
2800
ARCADE
OFFICES

COURTYARD

FFL

MAX. DEPTH 14.400m

Annual Operating Cost
£/m2 Gross

Typical Commercial Air Con. Office — Measured

BRECSU Good Practice — Measured

Milton Park Passive Solar Project — Predicted Using Dynamic Thermal Analysis

0   10   20   30   40   50
£/m2

1991 Figures

Heating   Electricity
Maintenance   Depreciation

based management team and through independently undertaken post-occupation surveys of particular new buildings. On a more formal basis, we undertake an annual Milton Park census of the views of building occupiers. The company spends time with prospective new occupiers to understand their requirements and establish whether these are best suited initially through existing space, or by constructing new buildings.

Generally, occupiers ask for good natural light (without solar glare) and expect natural ventilation, but the majority do not ask for full air-conditioning. At Milton Park there are only two whole buildings (totalling just under 1200m²) into which comfort cooling has been installed by Lansdown. However, there is a fully air-conditioned building occupied by the computer company Research Machines of some 5100m², but here the air-conditioning was installed by the occupier at their cost. The flexibility incorporated in the design of this building emphasizes that new buildings should provide an upgrade path in the event that mechanical ventilation or air-conditioning is required for specific office areas in the future or for specific clients (where air-conditioning is provided initially it may be prudent to provide a downgrade path).

3.3 *New Mill House,
183 Milton Park,
Oxfordshire. Architects;
RMJM.*

Concern for the wider environment

Milton Park is situated in the south Oxfordshire countryside, a location which is generally free of significant external noise and pollution. Although the Great Western Railway mainline is on the south side of the park, this causes only intermittent noise. The pleasant setting has encouraged us to develop the estate in as rural a character as commercial conditions allow. Car parks are well screened, buildings designed wherever possible using natural materials (such as brick), and planted open space between the buildings encourages contact between the inside and outside.

Our concern for the husbandry of the environment at Milton Park from green perspectives led us to explore the benefits of sustainability in the design of buildings. We also felt a responsibility to set an example.

Long-term flexibility

Since Lansdown retains ownership of its buildings it has an interest in their success in the long term. Buildings may be used for a wide range of purposes and by many different occupiers during their life. Occupiers frequently move within the park and it is important that there is flexibility in the size, use, quality and distribution of the stock.

We are particularly mindful as major property owners of the implications of the Global 2000 Report in 1980, the Brundtland Report in 1987, and the Rio Earth Summit of 1992. We seek to meet and where possible exceed government legislation, providing a more productive and environmentally friendly workplace for employers and their staff than competitors.

The recent changes to Part L of the Building Regulations and the proposals that were made in 1993 to limit the use of air-conditioning highlight the desirability of explaining the potential benefits of green buildings to occupiers. Our incorporation of simple passive solar design and other energy-saving features is both legislation, and occupier-led. Lansdown believe that increased fuel costs, possible carbon taxes in the future, and widespread concern for the environment will lead to an increased adoption of naturally ventilated buildings for most offices outside city centres.

These factors have encouraged the company to explore low-energy design for nearly a decade. There have been market benefits, but also a sense that developers have a responsibility to innovate in the area of sustainability. The construction of buildings which consume less energy has advantage for occupiers but, when coupled with the provision of buildings that aim to be the most productive premises from which companies of all sizes can operate, the ethos of environmentally friendly design enhances the reputation of the developer and the business park.

Inspired by the example of the NFU Mutual and Avon Group HQ at Stratford-upon-Avon (design by RMJM) Lansdown started in the 1980s to explore mixed-mode concepts of office design in collaboration with the building scientist William Bordass. New companies wishing to locate at Milton Park and Lansdown took the opportunity to explore how offices could be more productive, pleasant and energy efficient. Simple energy conservation had now expanded into a wider concern for environmental conditions and user comfort. Three significant new buildings resulted from this review: New Mill House (183 Milton Park), Marston Book Services (160 Milton Park) and the Business Campus (90–92 Milton Park).

New Mill House, 183 Milton Park, occupied by Research Machines

Research Machines' brief in 1989 was for a 4090m^2 (44 000ft^2) production/warehouse-type building completed as a shell finish with a clear height of 7.5m. The company also required 1020m^2 (11 000ft^2) of fitted open-plan offices, but wanted the whole building to have an unrestricted B1 planning use. Research Machines was particularly keen that the office area should be thermally efficient and effectively address the impact of solar gain without the use of air-conditioning.

Under the direction of partner David Lloyd Jones, RMJM produced a flexible design which included a courtyard

Table 3.1 Reasons for adopting sustainable commercial building design by Lansdown Estates

---

- long-term financial viability;
- concern for user needs, and comfort and health in the workplace;
- interest in wider environmental issues and the need to set a 'green' example;
- long-term flexibility in the use and provision of buildings, particularly with regard to energy costs and availability of affordable space;
- perceptions of market advantage through environmentally friendly design.

(21m x 11m) behind the initial offices to enable the office area to be extended northwards to meet changes in operational requirements. The office area incorporated an arcade at ground level with solar shading at first-floor level and conventional fenestration designed to give good opportunities for natural cross ventilation. The building was one of the first modern office buildings in England to positively address green principles and it is unfortunate that the subsequent computer equipment loadings in the office area proved to be three times the initial designed level with the result that three years after completion Research Machines installed air-conditioning. Without air-conditioning, the building completed in April 1991 cost £490/m^2 and has subsequently been adapted to provide a mezzanine level of offices in the former production area.

160 Milton Park, occupied by Marston Book Services

In July 1994 Marston Book Services came to us with a requirement for a new 5000m^2 (54 000ft^2) warehouse with 930m^2 (10 000ft^2) of ancillary offices. Lansdown had progressed its design thinking and David Lloyd Jones (now in practice as Studio E Architects) further developed the concept of modern non-air-conditioned commercial buildings specifically for Marston.[1]

The offices are arranged on two floors and incorporate various innovative features of sustainable design, including combined light shelves and solar screens, low-energy lighting

3.4 *Section, Marston Book Services Building, 160 Milton Park. Architects: David Lloyd Jones with RMJM.*

3.5 *Marston Book Services Building, 160 Milton Park. Architects: David Lloyd Jones with RMJM.*

and the positive use of thermal mass. The principal innovations at the Marston Book Services building are:

- An 'Interactive Window System' (developed with and now marketed by Colt International) to address the requirements for controlling the solar gain at the building edge, providing efficient natural ventilation, and also acoustic control. This is the first building in the UK into which this intelligent window system has been incorporated. The extra cost compared with ordinary windows was about £30 000.
- The ground-floor office ceiling incorporates egg crate tiles to enable advantage to be taken of the thermal capacity of the concrete planks which form the first

floor slab. The extra cost was about £1000. By exposing the concrete in this way it can effectively moderate peaks and troughs in temperature.

- The first-floor office uses a substantial central light well to enhance the amount of natural light while enabling summer temperature levels to be moderated by stack effect ventilation. The extra over cost compared with a plain roof ridge was about £27 000.

These three relatively straightforward features are complemented by energy saving solutions in the mechanical and electrical services, including low-energy lighting with movement detectors, anti-stratification fans in the warehouse, and radiator heating circuits compensated for external temperature.

3.6 *The Business Campus,*
90–92 Milton Park. Architect:
Nicholas Hare.

The green features were discussed and developed with Marston at the design stage and they positively welcomed the opportunity to enjoy a more natural working environment. Marston's directors and staff were subsequently briefed to help them to gain maximum advantage from the building's design features. An independent post-occupation evaluation has been undertaken by Building Use Studies, a London-based company specializing in monitoring the performance of buildings and feeding the results back to designers and their clients.

The building was completed on programme on 29 September 1995 at a cost of about £440/m², including fees.

The Business Campus, 90–92 Milton Park

The Business Campus consists of three buildings designed to suit a range of business uses, including office, production, laboratory, and research and development. They each incorporate green features and gave Lansdown the opportunity to explore the potential of recycling. The site was formerly occupied by three ordnance buildings which were demolished and provided a large amount of crushed concrete for fill and aggregate. This simple measure saved about £50 000 and greatly reduced the need for polluting lorry movements through Milton Park and adjoining areas.

The new buildings are each two storey, the smallest being 1700m^2 and the other two (which have atria) some 3100m^2 each. The larger buildings have a width of 12m either side of a 12m wide light well making an overall width of 36m. For users an acceptable working environment is achieved with openable windows on the external facades, producing cross ventilation through the space to the central light well where a high-level fan-assisted extract duct is located. However, other uses, particularly with partitioning around the perimeter of the light well, may require additional means of introducing fresh air to the deep-plan areas, particularly of the ground floor. A simple cost-effective ground cooling method was designed by Nicholas Hare Architects and the M&E consultants Hoare Lea & Partners. A ventilation system which made the most of the embodied energy of the ground below the building was developed. It is estimated that the ground temperature at the level of the pipes under the floor slab is generally constant at around 14–160°C. When the external air temperature varies by more than 50°C either side of this then either useful heating or cooling is expected to take place.

The system developed by Hoare Lee will rely upon fresh air taken in at the roof plant room level and ducted down risers to be passed through standard Hepsleeve ceramic pipe ducts some 750mm below the slab. The cooled fresh air is then introduced via floor channels into the ground floor. The system also serves the deep-plan sections of the first-floor area, when air is introduced into the raised floor void with the aid of a small fan and heater battery.

The principle of ground cooling with ceramic pipes has been successfully employed by Von Scholten in the Lessor office project at Gydevang on the outskirts of Copenhagen and similar installations have been used for offices and residential projects in Germany where very little heating is required in winter.

The initial cost of the underground pipework for this system is about £60 000 and this has to be considered in relation to future savings in energy consumption and the likely costs of air-conditioning plant in a more conventional building.

Conclusion

Lansdown is convinced that the green measures it has taken account for the fact that Milton Park enjoys a higher than average letting rate, currently 90%. The company believes that success in the future will be centred on:

- providing value for money for occupiers through green measures;
- maintaining accessibility by both public and private transport, and taking advantage of nearby rail links;
- reducing fossil fuel energy costs by working with natural forces and renewable sources of energy;
- making provision for young companies by providing flexible environmentally friendly workspace;
- providing flexible and responsive space by exploiting environmental and low-energy design.

Reference

1. Articles on the building can be seen in *CIBSE Journal*, December 1995, and *Architecture Today*, January 1996.

Graham Francis,
Sheppard Robson

4.1 *Detail of triple-glazed facades. Helicon Building, London. Architects: Sheppard Robson.*

The relevance of green buildings to the procurement and marketability of offices

My position as a member of the Technical Affairs Committee of the British Council for Offices (BCO) and as a partner at the London office of architects Sheppard Robson provides a good base from which to explore the relationship between green design and the marketability of offices. There is an obvious correlation between procurement policy, the level of specification, sustainability, cost and marketing. From a practical point of view, all green office development needs to be viable within market constraints; offer value for money, especially where new and relatively untried technologies are being employed; and provide genuine reduction in running costs.

Property development is a hard-headed business, particularly now when so much surplus office space exists. However, few developers construct green offices simply because of a hunch that there is money to be made from sustainability. Most property companies invest in green buildings for both long-term financial and ethical reasons; they feel that sustainable development and positive environmental management carry moral connotations with which they empathize. When, in terms of global warming, the ecological footprint of London is the size of the UK, we cannot continue with over-specified, poor energy performance offices.

Definition of the green office

It is important to define what we mean by the term green offices. The typical green office today has some or all of the following features:

— natural cross ventilation or mixed mode;
— natural daylight;
— sophisticated shading devices for solar control;

4.2 *Facade detail, Helicon Building, London. Architects: Sheppard Robson.*

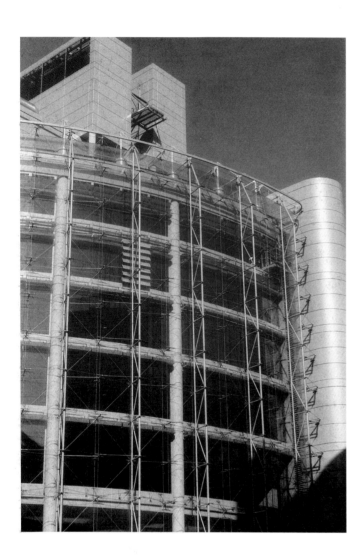

threats invalidate openable windows. Few urban sites provide the freedom to manipulate orientation for energy purposes and there is often overshading, which reduces the effectiveness of windows for interior light. Solar shading in urban areas tends also to provide perches for pigeons and starlings, which then soil the building facade reducing the effectiveness of windows and spoiling the appearance of the building. At Sheppard Robson's Helicon office building in the City of London, built in 1995 for Manchester Assurance, the latter problem was overcome by placing the solar blinds within a triple-glazed facade – the outer pane also provides further sound and thermal insulation and allows us to exploit the thermal flue effect at the building perimeter.

Highly glazed facades can be an attractive letting feature on offices as long as they do not lead to overheating, or become shabby through poor maintainance. Generally speaking, clear glass buildings allow improved contact with the outside and thereby enhance the office workers' sense of environmental wellbeing. Managers are increasingly recognizing the benefits of the naturally lit office to worker productivity and the psychological advantage of greater contact with the exterior environment.

The green investor

The green office requires a client willing to invest in new environmental technologies, happy to agree standards and environmental objectives above the regulatory minimum, able to take a long-term view of building investment, and willing to design for flexibility. In modern offices up to 90% of staff move location or adapt their workstation to new information technology each year. Sustainable design solutions need to integrate with facilities or building management – the eco-system of the office and the eco-system of the building must correlate.

For the developer, the sustainable office carries certain risks. In practical terms, for example, the green office requires:

–   more time for design;
–   the need to bring together appropriately skilled professionals;
–   the need to visit green buildings and become familiar with research reports;

–   good light distribution to the building core;
–   passive (i.e. user) controls;
–   thermal capacity dampening of structure;
–   stack effect ventilation incorporating atria;
–   displacement air-chilled ceilings;
–   upgradable base specification.

Needless to say, the typical green office (and many examples can be found in this book) encounters problems in urban sites where, for other sustainable reasons, the property industry is increasingly required to focus its attentions. City areas have poor air quality which undermines natural cross ventilation. The excessive noise and vandalism, and crime or bomb

4.3 *Broadgate Development, London, succeeds in creating good contact with the outside even in a city centre. Architects: Skidmore Owings and Merrill.*

4.4 *Judge Institute, Cambridge, demonstrates an unusual approach to green design in the education sector. Architect: John Outram.*

— the preparedness to take risks in developing new office prototypes;

— a proper understanding of the relationship between capital and running costs (in financial, energy and environmental terms).

There are complex financial balances to be struck, such as the consanguinity between facade costs and building servicing costs, or between Building Management System (BMS) costs and lighting costs. Normally (but not always) energy-saving technologies cost more in terms of capital costs than orthodox solutions, but they also save money in a predictable fashion. Understanding the balance of benefits is part of good green design.

Design implications

As a designer, I recognize there are problems which parallel those of the green client. While the architecture profession may wish to develop new approaches to sustainable development within the office or education sector there are constraints such as:

— time required for design in relation to client programme and fee;

— the risks and costs of innovation (especially against competitive fee scales);

— the need to develop and test prototypes;

- contractor/sub-contractor relationships and understanding;
- problems with certain contract forms (such as design and build);
- the need for feedback and monitoring to inform new projects;
- lack of coherent government incentives.

Both the design professions and BCO recognize the role of a softer green specification in bringing about a new generation of affordable, environmentally friendly office buildings. In 1994 the BCO introduced a new value-for-money standard office specification following a conference in Bristol. It sought to reduce costs and bring about a revival of the speculative office market based upon a new value-for-money bench mark of quality. The office building was no longer to be invariably air-conditioned with over-specified facilities, but naturally-lit and ventilated, solar protected, and lower cost (both running and capital). As companies downsized in the 1990s there was overwhelming evidence that differently configured, more flexible and cheaper offices were needed. Energy efficiency fitted remarkably comfortably into the new paradigm and before long the sustainable office had taken on a virtue none of us had anticipated a decade ago.

In terms of CO_2 emissions the rural footprint needed to deal with city energy use is in area terms in relationship of 1 to 25. Many in the property industry are beginning to take positive environmental action by insisting upon incorporating energy saving measures. In my experience, they are driven as much by the need to conserve the planet as the imperative to save money. Buildings are resources of materials and energy that pass through generations of owners and occupiers – and hence a long-term view of environmental problems is increasingly prevalent.

The urban site

There are many examples today of sustainable office buildings constructed on greenfield sites, but still relatively few in urban areas. The city-centre office building poses particular problems and it is rarely possible to adopt ecological principles to the same degree. The urban site is often polluted, contaminated, overlooked and dangerous. Natural ventilation is replaced by the mixed mode system where cleaned (but not necessarily clean) air is pushed around using an atrium to aid circulation.

The Helicon Building, with floorplates 2175m² in area, uses this system. It is highly glazed to allow for maximum use of daylight (lighting can be indirectly responsible for up to 60% of energy costs in a typical city office). Solar screens that double as light shelves prevent excessive heat build-up and deflect daylight at relatively even distribution into the centre of the building. A similar project in George Street, Croydon, integrates mechanical and engineering services with the structure using thermal mass to cool internal air temperatures, and a similar system of thermal flues to create a third glazing layer to form an insulating jacket around the building. This extra perimeter skin is used in summer to draw the heat out of the building by stack-effect and in winter to protect it from the cold.

When in 1994 the BCO introduced its new lower specification for urban offices it was to redefine the level of specification appropriate to the needs of most office occupiers incorporating the ability to upgrade the performance of the building if required, during its life. The idea was a kind of 'long-life, loose-fit, low-energy' specification which offered flexibility for localized or more comprehensive performance enhancement at a later stage. In theory it is possible to move from the BCO basic specification to full air-conditioning without great disruption. By using high floor-to-ceiling heights, sensible floorplates (13.5–18m deep), a high percentage of external glazing, and largely open plans, the new office of the 1990s offered cost benefit advantages over its counterparts of the 1980s while also being less environmentally damaging.

Compiling the brief

A key to green office design lies in agreeing the brief and producing a clear statement of project objectives by the client and full design team. There are a few guiding principles, but often each project has to develop its own characteristics from local conditions. For example, Rab Bennetts' office building for John Menzies near Edinburgh placed the spaces that had special environmental needs at one side of the building away from the main office areas. Here they could exploit passive principles more readily and provide the specific ambience needed by the client. In effect, the building adopted a pragmatic approach to natural ventilation: different parts of the building are dealt with environmentally in different ways.

With a specific client in mind, either as developer or tenant, it is easier to compile the brief from a green

4.5 *Base specification for green office. Architects: Sheppard Robson*

4.6 *Environmental principles of green office design. Architects: Fitzroy Robinson & Partners.*

Floor to floor section: the base specification

Key design points

- Opening windows, natural ventilation.

- Interstitial blinds, solar control.

- Exposed concrete soffit, night cooling.

- Uplighter as element of furniture, not fitting.

- 350 raised floor, cable management

- Radiator heating.

4.7 *Section, Helicon Building,*
London. Architects: Sheppard
Robson.

perspective. Most clients require measurable benefits from sustainable design, not merely environmental platitudes. Such measures do not have to be solely financial, many developers recognize the health, comfort and productivity advantages of a more natural building. In addition, some also value the contribution the building makes to the reduction of global problems – but only in as far as these benefits can be measured and used in the promotion of the development or company image.

Sustainable design involves greater risk (financial and professional) than conventional approaches. It requires more attention to detail, but the benefits of a successful green building outweigh the dangers. Working with some local authorities a green developer may be more likely to obtain planning consent and relaxations under building regulations. Green buildings

are more likely to comply with longer-term changes to environmental legislation thus retaining their value. With the current focus upon brownfield rather than greenfield sites, a developer reusing a contaminated inner site for sustainable development may well attract grants as well as concessions over land use or building height. For the architect, too, a green building design will keep the practice at the leading edge of change, which may attract further work and exposure in the professional journals.

We are at an interesting stage in the development of green architecture. There are many prototypes around, but when monitored they frequently do not behave as predicted. Sheppard Robson's Helicon Building (designed with services engineers Ove Arup and Partners) incorporates the flexibility

4.8 *Helicon Building, London: note how each facade varies according to orientation. Architects: Sheppard Robson.*

of layout and design that allows modification if the performance is not what we expect. Our client has taken a risk, especially on the facade, which as an element of construction cost about 25% more than the norm for office buildings in Central London. The justification is a combination of energy conservation and sound insulation as the site is an island surrounded by heavy traffic. On cost grounds, Helicon shows some remarkable economies. Energy running costs are about £50/m^2 per year which is significantly less than that of conventional office buildings. In a sense Sheppard Robson turned the site problems to sustainable advantage. The building is an example of mixed-use development with a four-storey Marks and Spencer shop, bank and lettable offices within a single building envelope.

A learning experience

Each green building is a learning experience for the developer, contractor and professional team. It is important that there is continuity between projects so that the lessons learned in one can be applied at the next. This requires leadership and commitment from the client, and knowledgeable and skilled professional advisers. Such understanding is rarely possible with certain contract forms since the fee scales and quality of construction often do not allow for innovation. Government procurement policy, rather than discouraging green building as it does at present, could set an example to the private sector.

The 1992 survey of office buildings and user needs by Richard Ellis and Partners (Chapter 2) opened up the

4.9 *Helicon Building, London: section through triple-glazed facade. Architects: Sheppard Robson.*

4.10 *Atrium, Helicon Building, London. Architects: Sheppard Robson.*

Table 4.1 Marketing advantages of green office buildings

– user satisfaction;
– benefits to health and comfort;
– company image;
– commercial advantage of environmental ethics;
– value for money in long term.

Table 4.2 Marketing disadvantages of green office buildings

– lack of consistent performance standards and feedback;
– lack of exemplar projects;
– complexity of comfort and control;
– limitations on cellular space;
– PC screen reflectance problems (with high daylight levels).

Table 4.3 Helicon Building, City of London: green principles

– mixed-use commercial development with large shop, bank and office;
– atrium to assist natural ventilation;
– triple glazing with ventilated cavity, integral solar shading and glare control;
– clear floor-to-ceiling glazing to maximize daylight penetration;
– solar controlled blinds which cannot be overridden;
– displacement air-conditioning which uses water-filled panels at ceiling level for cooling rather than VAV system. The system costs 15% more, but it should be 16% cheaper to run;
– balcony planted atrium to enhance psychological wellbeing

SUSPENDED CHILLED CEILING

STAINLESS STEEL TIE ROD

BOLT FIXED SINGLE GLAZED OUTER SKIN

450mm PERFORATED ALUMINIUM MOTORISED LOUVRES

DOUBLE GLAZED INNER SKIN

PERIMETER HEATING GRILLE

RAISED FLOOR

GALVANISED MESH WALKWAY

prospect of marketing green buildings as leading to greater consumer satisfaction and less absenteeism. The firm's research suggests that the costs saved by a company occupying a green building more than pay for the extra investment in sustainable design.

In the speculative office market it is particularly important that tenants understand the green intentions behind the building. The building manager has a key role to play in maintaining continuity between developer aspirations from a sustainable perspective and tenancy use of the building. This relates to controls and to wider philosophical issues. Green buildings need to be respected and appreciated for the values they represent by successive tenants. Active building management and the adoption of BRE's Toolkit for office operation encourage synergy between design and occupation. Where mutual understanding exists there is more likely to be the presence of a 'forgiveness factor' which allows tenants to accept wider variations in temperature than is the norm.

Conclusion

Green offices in cities have quite different characteristics from their counterparts in the countryside. Urban sites place obvious limitations on the use of natural ventilation, yet with modern technology it is possible to supplement passive solar principles with the more sophisticated solutions used by us at the Helicon Building and by Rogers' office at Daimler Benz in Berlin (Chapter 9). Many examples of green offices currently under construction (such as BRE's demonstration building near Watford, Chapter 11) are not appropriate for the urban situation. Offices in city centres, where generally speaking the market wants them, will cost more if constructed to green principles than those on business parks. The cost equation for green offices is not universally applicable – the extra cost gearing in cities will only be justified if there are tangible benefits to comfort, health, productivity and the psychological state of the office employee.

Chapter 5

David Partridge,
Argent Group

5.1 *The Governor's House, City of London: a green speculative office. Architects: Siddell Gibson.*

Achieving institutional levels of office design through sustainable approaches

Argent has an investment portfolio of offices worth £276m with property let mainly on long leases. The company owns and lets institutional property, much of it to companies of national or international standing such as British Telecom and Lloyds Bank. Our property programme is designed to have wide appeal across the property market. The issue of market appeal is the main justification for our approach to green design: we see the creation of sustainable, healthy buildings as providing a sound long-term investment with advantages over those of our competitors. This is not only true of Argent, but also of companies that have formed development partnerships with us, such as Citibank, Hypobank and the British Telecom Pension Scheme. Green design is about taking the long-term view — of opting for quality without over-specification. As owners of property, the Argent Group believe that performance flexibility linked to the sensible use of renewable energy (in daylight and passive cooling) provides greater robustness over the life of the building than the conventional view of the air-conditioned office.

Market appeal

Argent has reached the conclusion that while in the short term (up to ten years) green buildings often do not pay, in the longer term they do. Bridging these two time frames has proved difficult. An unknown occupier has unknown performance criteria and to appeal to the market our buildings need to offer the standard specification enjoyed by more conventional offices (i.e. air-conditioned). Argent's buildings are therefore flexible, high-performance and provide an air-conditioning path for different levels of occupancy. It is relatively easy to design green office buildings for known occupiers, such as RMJM's Scottish Office Building in Leith, Hopkins's Inland Revenue Building in Nottingham, and Foster's Mistral Building in the Thames Valley Park, but quite another story when you are building for the speculative market.

The problem for the property industry is that the standard, naturally ventilated or mixed mode atrium surrounded by a bank of relatively narrow office space does impose restrictions on office layout. The level of ventilation and the stack effect depends upon the effective use and management of the building. Tenants require as a matter of course a level of performance that tends to undermine the use of green office concepts. With energy costs relatively low (amounting normally to less than 1% of typical company outgoings) there is little incentive for the developer or tenant to opt for the green solution.

The Argent solution to speculative green design

Where competitors employ deep-planned, sealed office buildings with partial or full air-conditioning, Argent has developed high-performance offices for the institutional client which use:

5.2 *Section, One Brindley Place,*
Birmingham. Architects:
Anthony Peake Associates.

- solar, passive or mixed mode cooling;
- heavy masonry walls to moderate internal temperatures;
- openable windows with light shelves, solar screens and low E coatings;
- central atria with narrow floor plate perimeter offices;
- lighting controls which allow dimming from 500 to 350lux, and non-occupancy switch off;
- high structural floor heights (normally 4m).

Of course, not all these features are found in every building developed by Argent, but the company has a policy of environmental development linked to best practice guidelines. Each building learns from the experience of the one before: our developments at Brindley Place, on former derelict land in central Birmingham, have pushed at the frontiers of green office specification in an urban context; at the Thames Valley Business Park, near Reading, we have explored aspects of sustainable design more appropriate in greenfield settings.

Argent started exploring green speculative office development in 1990 in a project called Solaris in Basingstoke. The company looked at every possible avenue for green buildings; it produced impressive building sections with little arrows showing naturally ventilated air dutifully progressing around and graphs showing thermal lags between inside and outside tem-

perature and how night-time cooling used the thermal mass of the structure. For a brief period this project held the highest BREEAM rating ever awarded, though it was never actually constructed.

In 1991 the company became involved in a study group with the Department of Energy to explore passive solar design. We submitted one of our existing buildings, Temperway House, a fine example of 1970s architecture, to see whether one could actually convert it to green design principles. It had shallow plans (it was only about 12m wide) and working with the Short Ford Partnership we looked at ways of trying to cross-ventilate using thermal chimneys on the busy side so that there would be no necessity to actually open windows. Ideas were explored about using the thermal mass, stripping the building to expose the structure and cross-ventilating, but our tenant was unconvinced of the benefits and the project did not proceed.

The experience led us to the view that green offices potentially had benefits for both developer and tenant, especially when questions of energy use were widened to embrace other environmental issues. Today we are convinced that the comfort and health of office workers is best achieved through sustainable design principles, and this is reflected increasingly in tenant needs. From starting with energy as a prime factor in

5.3 a, b *Five Brindley Place,
Birmingham: top, perspective
by Jock Bevan to design by
Siddell Gibson; bottom, plan.
Architects: Siddell Gibson.*

a

b

5.4 *Solaris House, Basingstoke (project). Architect: David Partridge of Argent Development Corporation.*

shaping the design of offices, Argent has now moved to a wider environmental and ecological agenda.

Since Argent is a developer and owner of property the company has an interest in design and long-term asset strength as investments. Although Argent has constructed green offices (and is currently developing designs for several

others) it remains thwarted by the conventional institutional specification with its emphasis upon the sealed envelope, mechanical ventilation systems and artificial lighting. Many green clients, moreover, tend to commission their own buildings (British Gas, Chapter 7) rather than searching for office space within the speculative market. Whether this is through lack of availability of green offices or choice is a debate in which the industry needs to engage.

Conclusion

The circle of specification, product and demand is a vicious cycle of closed perceptions. The circle can be broken as Argent is doing by offering buildings that do everything required of the traditional specification, but at no extra cost to the tenant. For the developer, green buildings do not at present pay – energy costs are low and the relationships between environmental wellbeing and productivity in the workplace not yet fully appreciated.

Although green office buildings do cost more initially, the question for companies like Argent is whether they may be worth more in five or ten years time. The issue of enhanced value in the medium to long term, as environmental problems increase and resources become more scarce, is what drives Argent towards sustainable design.

Table 5.1 Comparative performance criteria for green and speculative offices

	A 'green' office building	A typical speculative office
Floor loadings	3.5kN/m²	4kN/m²
Lighting levels	350 lux	500 lux
Occupancy density	1 person per 14m²	1 person per 10m²
Small power loading	10–15W/m²	20–25W/m²
A/C upgrade to cope with additional cooling requirements	Some specialist areas	Additional 15W/m² over 30% floor area
Design temperature	Up to 26°C	21°C ± 1.5°C
Predicted number of working hours in excess of design temperature	10–20 hours	None
Floor depths	12–15m	Any
Ability to cellularize	10–15%	100%
Sub-divisibility of tenancies	Limited	Easier

5.5 *Thames Valley Park, Reading, development proposal by the Argent Development Corporation. The holistic nature of green development is evident in this model. Architects: Siddell Gibson.*

Table 5.2 Green speculative offices under construction in 1996 by Argent Development Corporation

Location	Cost	Architect	Green features
Birmingham			
Three Brindley Place	£12.5m	Porphyrios Associates	– doughnut-shaped floorplates (13.5m wide) – openable windows set in thick masonry walls
Four Brindley Place	£16.2m	Stanton Williams	– linear atrium – varied floorplates and size of accommodation to encourage mixed tenure – shaded glazing set in masonry walls – openable windows
Five Brindley Place	£14.5m	Siddell Gibson	– up-low ventilation system serving air at 18°C – 13m floorplate – openable windows
Reading			
Thames Valley Park	£14.2m	Siddell Gibson	– orientation for solar protection – heavy masonry wall on south side, lightweight wall on north side – openable windows

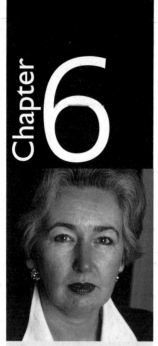

Chapter 6

Marilyn Standley,
Addison Wesley
Longman, now with
Chetterton Group

6.1 *Addison Wesley Longman
Building, Harlow, Essex.
Architects: Conran Roche
(now CD Partnership).*

Balancing human, energy and building costs

Rather than describe a building in detail, my chapter recounts the commissioning of a green office building from the perspective of a client. From 1991 to 1995 I was the project director on behalf of the Addison Wesley Longman Group for the new headquarters building at Harlow in Essex. Their previous building designed in the 1960s by Sir Frederick Gibberd was air-conditioned, inefficient and poorly regarded by staff. As a major publishing house, the group had specific needs for a combination of open-plan and cellular space, but above all the company needed modern, healthy office accommodation that fostered greater communication and creativity in staff.

Developing a people-centred brief

My task as project director was to help to evolve the brief, to liaise with the design team and contractor, and to create a building which satisfied Addison Wesley Longman's needs while also providing a sound investment for the company. For while the group required a new headquarters building, publishing is a volatile business and we had to be sure that the building could be let to a quite different company. In the event, soon after completion a third of the building was, in fact, rented by the supermarket group Tesco, and subsequently sold in total in the investment market with Addison Wesley Longman and Tesco remaining as tenants.

The brief evolved from two perspectives: the needs and preferences of the existing staff, and the perceptions of the property market in terms of sub-let tenancy requirements. Whereas most green buildings are for specific clients with distinctive needs, such as the PowerGen (Chapter 8) or Ionica Building, we structured the brief to allow for multi-occupancy. It was this factor which led to the division of each floor into six distinctive office areas divided by three atria on a linear configuration. The need for flexibility was vindicated when during the construction of the building the parent company Pearson restructured the business resulting in a surplus of 4000m² of office space (about 20% of total).

My role as project director for the new building took advantage of my background in facilities management. Addison Wesley Longman was keen that the new headquarters, expected then to cost about £21m, should reflect the needs of occupiers, i.e. the existing staff. In this regard the building is facilities management driven, but also shaped by user preference and market constraints. It is the combination of the three elements which made the brief for the Addison Wesley Longman Building different and which led to the construction of an office which is a departure from the norm.

Why build a green building?

As a publishing company there is little direct advantage in being 'green' from an image point of view (unlike The Body Shop or PowerGen), but there are many advantages in being green from the point of view of building running costs and staff productivity. The company has a higher than average usage of IT, which has implications for heating and ventilation, and which in turn helped to shape environmental thinking.

We had a site in mind not far from the existing building in central Harlow. It was not ideal but workable: a railway line to the north and busy road to the south determined the alignment on a north/south axis whereby the building had views eastwards over a nearby park.

The building was to be a marriage between site needs and people needs – but people came first. We undertook surveys and interviews with existing staff and quickly evolved the bones of the brief from the point of view of the people who make the business work. The brief sought a sensible balance between energy costs (which are usually fairly low) and people costs (which are normally fairly high). From the outset we tried to generate a brief which created the right working environment for people. That meant natural ventilation with windows that could be opened by the office staff themselves, plenty of daylight, views to the outside world, and a human scale for the workplace. Staff specifically expressed a wish to avoid air-conditioning and deep, characterless office areas.

It was clear from contact with staff representatives through our briefing teams that we needed to avoid the over-specification common to many other modern office buildings. We were fortunate in our choice of site: although environmental conditions were not ideal, they were not so poor that we had to seal the outside world from the inside. In fact, the vast

6.2 *Staff dining room, Addison Wesley Longman Building, Harlow. Architects: Conran Roche.*

6.3 *Contact with the outside is an important aspect of the Addison Wesley Longman Building, Harlow. Architects: Conran Roche.*

Environmental factors

The brief led to a functional analysis tempered by environmental factors, not merely the priorities of space planning. With human and environmental considerations to the fore and a site that gave access to cycleways, a park and a railway station, the framework existed for a new type of office for the company which had much in common with the 1990s generation of office buildings described elsewhere in this book.

With the Latham Report emerging at about the same time, which called for closer links between design professionals and the construction industry, we were keen to appoint the design team and contractor early on to encourage an integrated team approach. We appointed the CD Partnership (formerly Conran Roche), because of their design style, flexibility, and experience of working within new towns (Harlow was one of the first generation of post-war new towns). The CD Partnership helped to develop the feasibility study and was subsequently appointed to act as architect for the building and its fit-out. Other key consultants were EC Harris Project Management, and services engineers Cundall Johnston and Partners. ECD Architects carried out the BREEAM assessment and the design achieved 20 credits out of a possible total of 21.

With innovative buildings a non-adversarial team approach is important. The brief was subsequently developed by user groups that crossed functional and hierarchical boundaries. Several sub-briefs were prepared for specific aspects of the building or for special problems such as IT integration, workspace environment, corporate areas and site services. Each analysis of need was undertaken via the same framework:

- consultation;
- project board;
- project manager;
- user groups;
- professional team.

The importance of user groups

The inclusion of user groups in the functional analysis ensured that environmental and staff workplace needs were taken into account. Green architecture is a symptom of enlightened patronage and by giving prominence to staff needs, the green dimension arose naturally. It also meant that users of the

majority of staff expressed a preference for opening windows, views and contact with nature.

The brief was not long and dealt rather more with principles than with detail. Its main elements were for a building which was:

- responsive to different management needs;
- flexible, especially with regard to IT use;
- encouraging to teamwork;
- easy to maintain;
- cheap to run;
- low-energy in design;
- environmentally friendly;
- a pleasure to be in.

6.4 *Human scale and good diffused lighting characterize the office environment in the Addison Wesley Longman Building, Harlow. Architects: Conran Roche.*

building had a stake not only in its evolution but in its operation. Stake-holding is important especially when the 'forgiveness factor' comes into play if the building fails to perform exactly as predicted.

Typically in a company such as Addison Wesley Longman's 75% of its total costs are in staff salaries. Anything the business can do to make staff more productive and to reduce absenteeism through illness pays dividends. Staff costs far exceed energy building costs so user contentment is more important to the employer than good environmental design. However, what this building shows is that by involving staff in the generation of the brief the framework for design evolves from the joint perspectives of good management practice and low-energy design. For a healthy and satisfying workplace is invariably one which is energy efficient and productive.

6.5 *One of three atria providing solar-assisted ventilation at the Addison Wesley Longman Building, Harlow. Architects: Conran Roche.*

Drawing up the design plan

Staff expressed a preference for a human-scaled workplace and this suited our energy strategy. Rather than create one large, single entity building, the Addison Wesley Longman office consists of six work areas per floor (some open plan, others cellular), each divided by vertical circulation areas or atria. There are three atria to each floor arranged in linear form to separate the 13.5m deep office areas. Both atria and floorplates are similar in width with the two 90m long offices divided into three units by solidly expressed core and stair towers. Perceptually the plan allows each 13.5m x 30m unit of office accommodation to be read as a self-contained part, each with its own energy controls at the command of users. As the building is five and, in the centre, six storeys high, the subdivision of the office areas into fairly small units adds significantly to the arrangement whereby there are in total 72 separate heating and ventilation zones. The advantage is that fine tuning can occur to suit user or tenant needs, and that the areas requiring special environments, such as the restaurant and print room, can have their own energy strategy.

In a building of 16 000m² there is sense in breaking down the scale. This not only gives staff a feeling of belonging to a defined area of territory, but the smallness of the parts creates a greater sense of teamwork and engenders collaboration in the way our previous amorphous office never did. The three atria serve a distinct function – they are social and meeting spaces, their openness generates interaction between teams (so important in publishing where creativity is particularly valued), and the central atrium acts as an entrance space. In these senses we ensured that the environmental strategy for the building reflected closely the management strategy.

Controlling light and ventilation

The building is arranged with shared facilities on the ground floor (café, print room) and top floor (restaurant, board room, meeting rooms). Both top and bottom floor have views over terraces or gardens to the wider landscape. By separating these two most heat intensive floors the linking atria effectively builds up enough stack effect to naturally ventilate the office areas. The use of high-level manually opened windows, tall ceilings, exposed *in-situ* concrete structure, external solar screens and internal blinds effectively minimize summer heat gain. In winter when office windows are not likely to be opened, heat is provided by perimeter radiators and ventilation via ducts in the 300mm raised floor.[1] Energy saving is also achieved with the use of a lighting control system which switches uplighters off when daylight is sufficient or when offices are unoccupied.

As with many office buildings, the external control of sunlight supplements daylight penetration through reflective louvres. Daylight is maximized by the use of exceptionally large windows and white-painted concrete structure. The sunlight shades are part of an integrated facade system developed by Schüco which consists of five main parts:

6.6 *Ground floor café, Addison Wesley Longman Building, Harlow. Architects: Conran Roche.*

- top section of clear, double-glazed, inward-opening windows with etched glass to reduce glare;
- external aluminium curved louvres of varying depth to suit angle of incidence;
- middle section of clear double-glazed outward-opening windows;
- lower section of fixed double-glazed windows;
- bottom section of polyester powder-coated insulated aluminium panel with integral 100mm foil-backed insulation.[2]

By setting the glazing deep within the structural frame high sun shading is provided for the top window panel, while the external louvres protect the two lower windows. The arrangement is energy efficient and gives control of ventilation to users without obstructing views.

Unusually for such buildings, the atria are not roof but mainly wall-glazed. Light enters the three atria spaces predominantly via walls of glass, which project through the roof of the building. Energy modelling at the design stage confirmed that good light penetration and natural ventilation could be achieved without roof-top glazing. The central atrium has a solid roof and the north and south atria have circular rooflights punched through the concrete. Perimeter wall glazing of the atria avoids the problem of solar shading the rooftop (Daimler Benz, Chapter 9) and allows daylight to wash down the interior walls without glare.

Conclusion

Built at a cost of £21m the Addison Wesley Longman Building is 5% more economical than the norm (the final cost was £1073/m^2 in 1995) though with higher external envelope costs.[3] Additional costs associated with thermal massing were approximately £13/m^2 and roof planting about £8/m^2.[4] However, the use of exposed concrete rather than suspended ceilings resulted in a saving of £20/m^2 and energy running costs are about 35% that of comparable air-conditioned offices.

The Addison Wesley Longman Building is a user-led reaction against the anonymous, deep-plan office of the 1980s. We set out to achieve a healthy, responsive, low-energy new headquarters building that was easy to understand and not over-elaborate in operation. With between 15% and 30% of

Table 6.1 Addison Wesley Longman Building, Harlow: main green features

- 80% of staff expressed preference for opening windows;
- large office divided by atria into small working areas;
- elaborate facades with integral solar screens and large opening windows;
- high ceilings and exposed concrete structure (columns and ceilings) for thermal capacity;
- three atria of different form for energy reasons;
- design evolved in close collaboration with users;
- building divided into 72 heating and ventilation zones, most under individual control;
- semi-urban rather than rural site within walking distance of railway station;
- lighting control system related to daylight quality and room occupancy.

the office space on any one floor as cellular accommodation at any one time we also had to ensure that there was flexibility in terms of energy operation.

We did not set out originally to produce a 'green building': the environmental dimension grew as we consulted with staff and looked seriously at the health, maintenance and energy costs of a typical air-conditioned office block. When we asked staff initially to list the eight features they most desired in the new building; 80% opted for opening windows. It was this decision, which, more than any other, shaped the design and which with post occupancy surveys has led the users to express pleasure in working in the building. Pleasure, job satisfaction and productivity go together and justify the energy strategy in more than fiscal terms alone.

References

1. Details can be seen in *The Architects' Journal*, 30 May 1996, p. 28.
2. Ibid, p. 32.
3. *The Architects' Journal*, 30 May 1996, contains a full cost breakdown.
4. Ibid, p. 30.

PART 2

Case studies
of best practice

Ken Shuttleworth,
Foster and Partners

7.1 *Lycée Albert Camus,*
Fréjus, France. Architects:
Foster and Partners.

Mistral Building, Reading

The practice of Foster and Partners has been designing low-energy office buildings for several years, especially in Germany and France where green thinking is more advanced than in the UK. Commerzbank in Frankfurt is an example. To explain the background to Foster and Partners' offices for British Gas in the Thames Valley Park, near Reading, Berkshire, due for completion in 1997, it is worth looking first at the Commerzbank Building and other developments in Europe.

Commerzbank, Frankfurt, and other European projects

Constructed in 1997, Commerzbank is the first high-rise, naturally ventilated building in the world. The bank is triangular in plan, two sides are offices and the third a garden enclosed within an atrium rising through 60 storeys – the height of the building. The differential temperature between inside and outside air pressure provides cross ventilation for the offices.

The atrium is a key element of the design. The four-storey high gardens corkscrew around its edge deflecting air movement in response to different wind direction. Every ninth floor the atrium is sealed to stop the build up of an excessive stack effect throughout the full height of the building. The combination of radiant cooling, opening windows and an environmentally efficient plan form allows the tower to achieve remarkable energy performance.

The Frankfurt office building owes the direction of its innovation to a school the Foster office designed at Fréjus in the South of France. Known as Lycée Albert Camus it, too, was naturally ventilated with fresh air taken between a double skin roof constructed of two layers of concrete and lightweight steel. The thermal capacity of the concrete roof moderated the temperature to the point where, with solar shading on the

7.2 *Micro-electronic Centre,*
Duisburg. Architects: Foster
and Partners.

cooling in the ceiling, trickle ventilation and a triple-glazed external skin that takes away the heat as it hits the glass wall to the top of the building, the Duisburg buildings have proved to have a zero energy bill.

The Mistral Building for British Gas

At Reading, Foster and Partners' task was to design an energy efficient office for British Gas on a site bounded to the south by a railway line and noisy access road. The attractive views were to the north over a park and the River Thames. We located the Mistral Building, as it became known, to the northern edge of the site where the environment was better, aware that it would expose the south elevation to potentially difficult problems of solar gain and internal glare.

The design was evolved to mitigate these problems without resorting to the high environmental costs associated with totally sealed offices, which was the solution adopted by most other architects at the Thames Valley Park. It seemed natural to us to develop a design in a parkland setting that brought the external environment to the centre of the building through the use of naturally ventilated, shallow-plan built forms. The strategy was to have four fingers of buildings 16.5m wide penetrating into the park with curved ends against the river. This allowed us to locate the plant rooms on the south side providing useful solar protection. Part of the environmental strategy developed with building services engineers Roger Preston and Partners also involved placing the buildings and lake in close proximity in order to use the chilling effect of air passing over water.

As the scheme for British Gas evolved, the four fingers of accommodation were pushed out as peninsulas towards the lake with the water also brought partly inside the building. Car parking was placed on the south side where it was hidden from inside the building by the plant rooms, with toilets and staircases placed as solid stone walls on that elevation. The largely solid south elevation contrasts with the mainly transparent north where clear glazed walls provide good views over the parkland. The finger concept brings the perception of the external environment and its physical benefits into the heart of the building. Dividing the building into fingers and cores allows for phased construction: two fingers and a linking atrium have recently been constructed so we can monitor energy performance before completing the whole project.

south side, the school remained cool even in summer. The trick is to keep the air moving by establishing thermal currents within both the building itself and through the structure of walls and roof.

Another French design by the practice, an office for EDF (the national electricity grid company in France), exploits internal chimneys to draw air in from the perimeter. By placing the chimneys in the centre of the building and employing extensive external shading, constructed in this case of locally grown timber, the air goes between the layers of the external cladding pulling in fresh cool air from outside. As with the school, the orientation of the building in relation to wind, sun and shading was crucial.

Zero energy bill at Duisburg

A group of business park buildings constructed between 1992 and 1994 by Foster and Partners at Duisburg in Germany explored the potential of co-generation where gas is burned to make electricity and provide winter space heating. Based on combined heat and power (CHP) principles, about half the electricity produced powers the building, the remainder is sold at a profit to the national grid. In conjunction with the use of absorption chillers, which convert sunlight into coolth, radiant

7.3 *Mistral Building, Reading.*
Architects: Foster and Partners.

7.4 *Site plan, Mistral Building,*
Reading. Architects: Foster and
Partners.

Mistral Building, Reading

7.5 *Cross section through atrium, Mistral Building, Reading. Architects: Foster and Partners.*

7.6 *Ground floor plan of phase one, Mistral Building, Reading. Architects: Foster and Partners.*

7.7 *Long section through atrium, Mistral Building, Reading. Architects: Foster and Partners.*

7.8 *Cross section, Mistral Building, Reading. Architects: Foster and Partners.*

7.9 *Detail showing natural ventilation and exposed concrete soffits with integral lighting, Mistral Building, Reading. Architects: Foster and Partners.*

Ventilation

As with all green buildings, the cross section is as important as the plan – arguably more so. The 16.5m deep offices obtain their ventilation via opening windows which exploit the differential air pressures set up by the atrium and inside/outside conditions. Windows are designed so that flaps open at night to cool the structure. By using an exposed concrete ribbed floor structure the offices exploit cooling, particularly at the edge of the building where the ribs extend as cantilevers outside the glazing line. The high thermal mass of the concrete frames and the deliberate policy of leaving the structure exposed to the internal and external air, provide an effective low-energy means of moderating internal temperatures. In extreme weather conditions, however, a mixed mode system operates.

The cantilevered structural edge extends 4.5m beyond the column line. The columns themselves are buried within the thickness of the partitions some way back from the glazing line, providing a column-free space in the centre and at the perimeter of the building. The concrete ribs on a 1.5m grid are expressed on the building facades providing architectural interest by day and night.

Cladding, glazing and lighting

The strategy of expressing the concrete ribs in order to exploit the high thermal mass of the building for radiant cooling influenced our thinking with regard to cladding. Since the building facades face in all directions our starting point was the design of the building envelope, which reflected the different performance needs of east, west, north and (to a lesser extent) south facades. We deliberately avoided using the same cladding design all the way around the building, developing virtually clear elevations on the north and east sides, and more solid panels on the west facades where the low afternoon sun posed difficulties. As noted, the plant rooms, lifts and services are generally placed on the south elevation providing the necessary solar protection.

We tested the glazing thoroughly before installation. Computer modelling and the construction of trial panels allowed the performance to be evaluated from thermal, acoustic, wind and pressure points of view. With innovative buildings it is better to test ideas on a rig rather than the building site. The glazing uses a different combination of clear, fritted and insulated panels according to orientation. The glazing, too, has different areas which can be opened according to aspect, and is designed so that air can circulate through the window itself, rather than from outside to inside.

The coffered floor slabs combine lighting in the form of uplighters which run around the inside of each coffer and reflect on a baffle. Lighting and structure are, as in most of our buildings, closely integrated. By being close to the concrete structure, the heat of the lights is absorbed rather than dissipated into the working environment.

Choosing natural materials

The Mistral Building achieved an excellent BREEAM rating. By providing measures such as bicycle sheds, water conservation measures, timber from sustainable sources and, of course, low-energy design, the building is among the top three or four in the country. However, while being green it is not devoid of

Table 7.1 Mistral Building, Reading: main green features

- building partly constructed below ground level;
- orientation for solar protection;
- distribution of service zones and circulation to south side for solar shade;
- high thermal capacity combined with transparency on north and east elevations;
- exposed concrete ribs for radiant cooling;
- fairly narrow plan depth (16.5m) combined with partial atria;
- timber from sustainable sources (beech and iroko);
- elevations which vary in transparency and insulation according to orientation;
- facade venting through cavity;
- openable windows;
- partial stack-effect ventilation;
- use of exterior lake for cooling.

architectural interest or bravado: on the contrary, the energy-saving measures give the building a distinctive aesthetic quality. The atrium in particular with its timber bridges and the staircase wrapping around a timber-clad lift shaft has a soft green feel which alludes to the parkland environment outside. The external wall goes all the way around the building, but also through the atrium where it does not change (as walls do in most atria) but remains the same thereby helping to explain the function of the atrium as a climate modifier.

The use of timber poses problems for architects today. Since hardwood forests are the world's major reservoirs of biodiversity and contribute significantly to the conversion of CO_2 into oxygen (and hence moderate global warming) the specification of hardwoods is fraught with difficulty. Foster and Partners consulted with BREEAM over the best species to use and chose Iroko from guaranteed sustainable sources. Timber is widely used as a finish: it is employed as flooring, as cladding on the bridges that criss-cross the atrium, and as an external canopy. Timber used in combination with natural stone on the perimeter walls and the practice's more usual high-tech finishes creates an atmosphere which is soft yet efficient. As an energy-efficient building, we endeavoured to use natural finishes to complement the natural ventilation and radiant cooling strategy.

7.10 *Use of sustainable hard-wood, Mistral Building, Reading. Architects: Foster and Partners.*

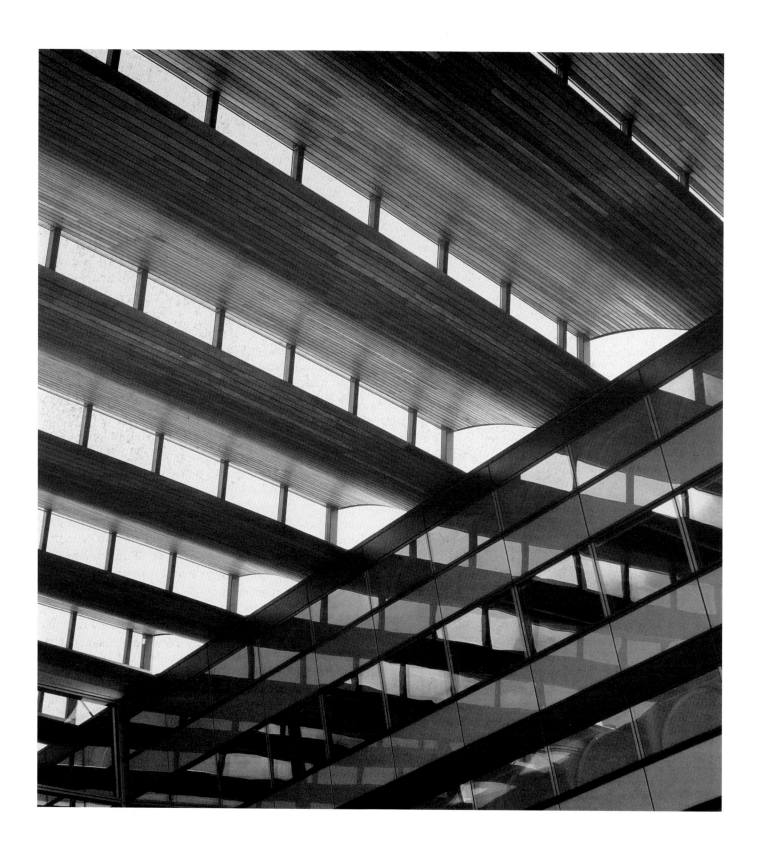

7.11 *Exterior view of entrance canopy, Mistral Building, Reading. Architects: Foster and Partners.*

We also used nature as a green metaphor. The choice of materials (greenish stone and green finished metal framing) creates a building which is green in both concept and appearance. This, added to the generous reinforcement of tree planting in the park, sets the building apart from its neighbours. Since the Mistral Building is partly buried in the ground (up to sill level) for energy saving purposes, the appearance is one of the ground plane of grass and shrubs entering directly into the building. When the ground-floor windows are opened, the view out over the blades of grass symbolically unites the building with the landscape.

Conclusion

British Gas commissioned us to design an energy-efficient office building, initially for their own occupation, but subsequently as a building that could be let to others. Our thinking in the design of the building moved outwards from energy performance to embracing wider environmental and ecological considerations under the influence of BREEAM. The site demanded a sustainable approach from masterplanning to the specification of materials.

It is difficult to say at this early stage whether the building pays in the full range of benefits and impacts involved. Certainly the energy bills will be only about 20% of those of a more conventionally designed office building. Although construction costs were slightly higher than the norm for speculative offices, the building represents for British Gas a symbol of its commitment as a major energy producer to environmental issues. At present energy cost levels, I would estimate that the pay back period is 12 to 15 years, though I like to think that the approach to the design from an environmental perspective adds value to the building, which would be reflected in any subsequent sale.

Rab Bennetts,
Bennetts Associates

8.1 *Office interior, PowerGen Building, Coventry. Architects: Bennetts Associates.*

PowerGen Building, Coventry

PowerGen is one of the three major electricity generating companies in England formed by privatization of the industry in 1990. The company appointed Bennetts Associates as architects in 1991 to design an initial scheme for its new headquarters in Birmingham because of the practice's 'analytical approach and experience with natural ventilation'.[1] After studying several possible sites, that at Coventry was chosen in 1992. The brief was for a low-energy building which optimized daylight and user control of the internal environment. PowerGen's brief did not stipulate natural ventilation, but left the design team to make proposals. However, they did not like air-conditioning and wanted to have opening windows.

The decision to construct a new building rather than rent existing floorspace was in order to pursue long-term operational efficiency linked to energy conservation. The building had to be able to accommodate around 600 staff under one roof, but without a hint of corporate extravagance. A single headquarters building held the prospect of operational integration and greater energy efficiency than had the building been split as earlier into separate units. The brief also required high levels of internal comfort without relying upon conventional control from a central plant room.

Evolution of the design strategy

The focus of design effort was upon the workplace and its environmental conditions rather than overt corporate or architectural image.[2] However, in evolving a design strategy, the importance of building or room shape, colour, daylight, views, circulation routes and meeting places emerged with greater force than in a conventional office building.[3] The analysis of client need showed that PowerGen's operations were best met by narrow width floorplates of six structural bays served by a circulation route on the long side. The design selected was

8.2 *Typical floor plan,*
PowerGen Building, Coventry.
Architects: Bennetts Associates.

Key
1   Office
2   Atrium
3   Service tower

4   Computer facilities
5   Restaurant
6   Servery
7   Kitchen

to use four such floorplates divided by a long central atrium stacked vertically into a three-storey building.

The orientation of the building helped to reduce solar gain and control glare from low sun angles. The PowerGen Building is on an east/west axis exposing one long elevation to the north and the other to the south. This orientation restricts the problem of glare and afternoon solar gain to east and west-facing glazed elevations. In restricting the area of glass on east and west facades by positioning the staff restaurant, conference area, plant rooms and air-conditioned communication rooms against the gables, the awkward low-angle sun was cost-effectively masked. Simple solar shading was required on the south elevation, however, but the relative expense was lower than with full air-conditioning.

No office building of this size can be totally free of mechanical ventilation. We sought at PowerGen to restrict air-conditioned areas to a minimum and to place such accommodation at opposite ends of the building where it could act as a buffer. In addition, the photocopiers and printers were located in air-conditioned business centres in line with the stair cores in the atrium, where they could act as a point of social contact. We also provided separate areas for computer suites, which needed mechanical ventilation, rather than design all the offices to such high standards.

Besides careful attention to the positioning of accommodation relative to orientation and ventilation load, we sought to maximize daylight penetration by restricting the floorplates to 12m in depth. As daylight maximization without sunlight on the workplane is crucial to low-energy design we evolved a

building section that optimized daylight opportunities from both the exterior and interior via the atrium. The two mainly open-plan office areas are divided by a linear atrium, which bisects the building on its long axis. The floorplates are identical on each of the three floors with only the configuration of the accommodation in the gables varying.

Maximizing the use of daylight

The basic arrangement eases shading requirements for the facades and optimizes the availability of diffuse sky-light.[4] This enters the building from the atrium where rooftop solar shading filters out direct sunlight except in specific areas where background brightness was desirable. Angled ceiling soffits in the atrium and glazed balustrading to the office areas allow a gentle glare-free transition from the bright and airy atrium to the working spaces. Daylight enters the office areas mainly from the north and south elevations and here lighting levels are evenly distributed throughout the building section. As with the light graduation from atrium to office areas, contrasts in the visual field at the perimeter are dealt with via a combination of external screening and daylight shelves.

The building footprint and cross section are designed to maximize daylight and to exploit natural ventilation through the stack effect, or via cross ventilation. These two priorities shaped many subsequent decisions, including the design of the windows. The windows extend from just above desk height to ceiling with a flush joint between the window head and structural soffit. The detail avoids glare and provides a better spread of daylight across the ceiling than with traditional window design. The windows are clear-glazed, double-paned, using low-E units, with upper panels of tinted glass to reduce sun transmission on the south elevation.[5] Each vertical panel of glazing is divided into three vertical units, the lower two being operated manually by users and the upper section linked to the Building Management System (BMS) for night-time chilling of the structure. This allows the users to choose a high or low level air-stream, according to external conditions. Glazing represents less than 50% of the total facade area.

Ventilation solutions

Both the open aspect of the site and the freedom to exploit orientation afforded advantages which the design of the building and its window systems exploit. The surrounding area provides a relatively quiet and clean environment, which we have sought to bring indoors via the atrium and large opening windows. Computer simulation confirmed that a combination of a long thin building with a three-storey sandwiched atrium would provide the natural ventilation and high quality environment required of the brief.

It was clear in the modelling of the building that with the exception of still days, cross-ventilation with such a shallow floorplate would be the dominant factor in moving air around the building rather than the stack effect. Only on windless days is the stack effect a major contributor to natural ventilation in a building of these dimensions. Detailed research into local weather conditions indicated that very hot days were never

still and that still days were generally experienced at modest temperatures. In consequence, the design team concluded that the convention of designing for a hot, still day was not applicable in this case.

Thermal mass is used to moderate internal temperatures. The concrete structure of round columns and coffered ceiling is left exposed in office areas in order to modify the interior climate. Night-time ventilation exploits the heavyweight *in-situ* construction to provide passive cooling during hot summer days. This has proved to be of critical importance in use.

The architectural benefits of coffered ceilings

Leaving the concrete structure exposed allowed us to take advantage of the architectural framework as the main ingredient of the tectonic experience. With no need to provide suspended ceilings except in a few dedicated areas of air-conditioning, the coffered ceilings and fair-faced concrete columns assume an important environmental and aesthetic role. As with much green design, the architectural benefits are an important by-product of sustainability.

The detailed design of the coffered ceiling is the result of many factors – structural, environmental, acoustic and visual. The raking of the structural coffers to the outer edge provides good daylight penetration; the elliptical profile avoids acoustic focusing; the optimum visual depth is sufficient to provide a clear span across the floorplate; and the suspended lighting

8.4 *Detail of window design and solar shading on south elevation, PowerGen Building, Coventry. Architects: Bennetts Associates.*

8.5 *View of atrium (left) and office area (right): note the timber solar screen. Architects: Bennetts Associates.*

Factors that determined the building's configuration

There is a delicate balance struck at the PowerGen Building between five inter-related factors:

- office floorplate to atrium width dimension;
- daylight penetration and solar gain;
- orientation of building;
- fabric heat loss;
- local environmental conditions.

These factors determined not only the size and shape of the building, but the floor to ceiling heights, the distribution of types of accommodation, and the choice and method of construction. Concrete was used for the structure because of its benefit over steel in terms of night-time cooling. *In situ* concrete, with a painted, high-quality finish, was cheaper and easier to detail than pre-cast concrete. Externally the building uses panels of brickwork for the same reason. The thickness of the concrete floor slab and its surface area is crucial to the use of thermal capacity for radiant cooling. Research suggests that the optimum thickness is between 150 mm and 190 mm with the first 50–70 mm being the most effective on a daily thermal cycle.[8] Post-occupancy analysis suggests that the coffered profile provides 2–3°C more cooling effect than a flat slab construction.

PowerGen forms a marriage between the functional needs of the company and its commitment to good environmental practice. PowerGen knew when we were appointed in 1992 that it had a particular type of desk configuration in mind. In effect, the company had an idea of the environmental and operational characteristics of the working environment. In fact, the function and organisation of the office space was dominant and hence the design evolved from the inside out. Our task was to develop a typical floorplate for 40–45 people (the maximum team size) and to test this against performance criteria – energy use, lighting, acoustic, circulation, flexibility, etc. We modelled the area using computers and made a physical mock-up which was assessed using light meters. This confirmed the environmental assumptions and the space syntax qualities of the building. Having perfected the floorplate diagram it was a short step to placing the heavily serviced accommodation at one end and the special 'hot spot' accommodation (copiers, fax machines, etc.) by the cores in the atrium.

boom uses the structural soffit to diffuse artificial light in an even fashion.[6] Ducts when they are needed are positioned in the 450 mm raised floors thereby avoiding compromise with the multifarious function of the ceiling.

Acoustic elements

There can be a conflict between thermal and acoustic design in offices with exposed structures. The exploitation of the thermal coefficient of exposed concrete construction readily leads to a noisy indoor environment. The answer at the PowerGen Building is to provide areas of sound-absorbent covering placed as wings on either side of the light fittings hung beneath the coffered ceiling. The acoustic material made from perforated metal filled with sound-absorbing mats soaks up sound on both the upper and lower surfaces, and therefore absorbs direct noise from the office workstations and indirect noise reflected off the concrete coffers.[7] With open-plan offices that use structural elements to moderate temperatures, it is important to integrate architectural, thermal, acoustic and lighting issues. Besides the combined light and acoustic fittings, we designed the shape of the coffers to absorb noise, the profile being elliptical not radial in cross section.

8.6 *Exposed concrete structure helps to stabilise temperatures, PowerGen Building, Coventry. Architects: Bennetts Associates.*

8.7 *Section through external wall of south elevation, PowerGen Building, Coventry. Architects: Bennetts Associates.*

Key: **1.** In-situ *concrete floor slab.* **2.** *Opening window on BMS for night-time cooling.* **3.** *Clear double-glazed windows with low-E units.* **4.** *Combined solar shading and daylight shelves.* **5.** *Combined heater sill.* **6.** *Raised floor.* **7.** *Brickwork panel.*

The company and design team (which included Ernest Griffiths & Sons as building services engineers[9]) were not just looking directly for a low-energy solution, but a building which offered environmentally something more than the standard office interior with its flat suspended ceilings and architecturally neutral spaces. The decision to expose the structure, to use narrow floorplates within a linear building, and to develop the long coffered ceiling profile led to an office building that looked rather like a solid warehouse structure from the 19th century. We rather like the way the PowerGen Building alludes to the industrial revolution in its imagery – after all it is merely a factory processing information.

The column-free interior of the offices makes for elegant spaces where the structural soffit and integral lighting and acoustic fittings are dominant. Today 95% of the staff at Power-Gen work in offices which have natural ventilation, access to openable windows, and views out to the sky and internally to the atrium.

Although the design evolved through three distinct stages, the shape and pattern of the floorplate remained the same. What did change was the relationship between the circulation areas and the floorplate, and the grouping of the floorplates relative to the atrium. By placing the cafeteria areas, computer suites and meeting rooms at the perimeter of the offices, we effectively screened the floorplates at the vulnerable east and west ends, and provided greater architectural modelling of the facades. A consequence of the design strategy is the greater exterior length than in an air-conditioned office, and the greater cost of the facade elements (because of solar screening and expensive glazing design). However, as an architect it seems better to invest in the architecture that people see rather than in the hidden services (as with air-conditioned buildings), which are of little aesthetic benefit and a short economic life.

Conclusion

PowerGen cost no more than a conventional office building, yet it uses only 40% of the energy load of air-conditioned floor space. With its opening windows and sense of the outside penetrating to the interior, the building is a model of the

8.8 *The energy planning of the PowerGen Building, Coventry, is clearly visible at night. Architects: Bennetts Associates.*

Table 8.1 PowerGen Building, Coventry: main green features

— 12m office floor plates;
— linear building with sandwich atrium;
— double-glazed top-opening windows with solar screening;
— arrangement of non-standard accommodation to provide solar screening buffer zones;
— deep coffered slab for radiant cooling;
— integral light fittings with sound absorbent wings;
— roof-vented atrium;
— integral window-head and ceiling for smooth daylight penetration;
— orientation of building to reduce low-angle sun penetration;
— heat-emitting office equipment placed in concentrated areas, with local A/C.

healthy, natural office of the future. Like many green designs today it owes a debt to Arup Associates' pioneering work, especially the Wiggins Teape Building in Basingstoke, and in its turn we have refined the PowerGen model at the John Menzies Building near Edinburgh.[10] Each building is a logical development of the former: each confirms that by taking a holistic view of architectural design, green buildings do in fact pay. The building was constructed at the modest cost in 1994 of £700/m² (about £900/m² fully fitted out), which is viable in terms of market rents and cheaper than an equivalent air-conditioned office.

References

1. *The Architects' Journal*, 2 March 1995, p. 44. This issue contains a detailed case study of the PowerGen Building.
2. Ibid.
3. Ibid.
4. Adam Jackaway and David Green, 'PowerGen in the light of day', *The Architects' Journal*, 11 March 1996, p. 46.
5. Ibid.
6. *The Architects' Journal*, 2 March 1995, p. 46.
7. Iain Clarke, 'Sounding out the soffit', Architects' Journal, 7 March 1996, p.44.
8. Alistair Blyth, 'Using the building fabric to balance energy demand', *Concrete Quarterly*, Spring 1996, p. 13.
9. Detailed case study of PowerGen services design, *CIBSE Journal*, March 1995.
10 Case study of John Menzies Building with article by Rab Bennetts on evolution since PowerGen. *The Architects' Journal*, 30 November 1995.

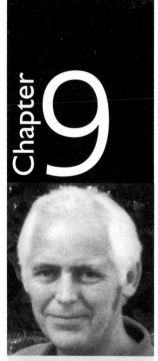

Lennart Grut,
Richard Rogers
Partnership

9.1 *Site plan, Daimler Benz*
Building, Berlin. Architects:
Richard Rogers Partnership.

Daimler Benz
Building, Berlin

In 1993 Daimler Benz AG appointed Richard Rogers Partnership to design three buildings – two office blocks and a residential block – which form part of the masterplan of the Potsdamer Platz development in Berlin designed by the Renzo Piano Building Workshop with Christoph Kohlbecker. The main entrance to the buildings faces onto Linkstrassen Park and the basic form of each building is based on a typical Berlin block with a centralized courtyard. District heating and district cooling as well as the main electric supply is supplied by BEWAG by means of CHP plant and absorption chillers.

This chapter concentrates on one of the Daimler Benz office blocks known as B6. The key objective was to design three buildings that would form a new European standard for the integration of low-energy design into architecture suitable for dense urban environments. Each building aims to optimize the use of passive solar energy, natural ventilation and natural light to create a comfortable and energy-efficient working environment.

Environmental strategy

The strategies adopted in the design of the office block are as follows:

- opening up the courtyard to optimize daylight penetration, improve passive solar gain in winter, and enhance views to the park;
- using an atrium to act as a thermal buffer, induce natural ventilation through the atrium and the building, and create a well-tempered entrance hall;
- using a high-performance building envelope to minimize conflicts between solar gain and daylight to 'fine-tune' the facades in response to solar exposure, and develop a

modular facade system which can be modified according to external conditions and user requirements;

— naturally ventilating the building throughout the year by using optimized window configuration and night-time free cooling.

Predicting the results

A well-designed daylit and naturally ventilated office building in Berlin will normally have an annual primary energy consumption of approximately 140 kWh/m². In comparison, an air-conditioned, standard office building with convention-

al services design and control could consume between two to five times more energy. Our target was to reduce the annual primary energy consumption of each office building to approximately 80kWh/m². Initial analysis indicated that each office block would consume approximately 35% of artificial lighting and 30% of heating and cooling energy normally used by a typical naturally ventilated office block in Germany.

Here follows a summary of the analysis undertaken by ourselves and building services engineers Schmidt Reuter and Partners of Hamburg in order to achieve the environmental objectives:

9.2 *Diagrammatic sections and plans showing relationship between daylight factor and built form, Daimler Benz Building, Berlin. Architects: Richard Rogers Partnership.*

Section 1

Section 2

— The building form was examined.
— The building envelope was analysed.
— The internal environment, including natural ventilation and daylight, was also examined.

Computer modelling techniques and physical models were used in the design process to integrate architectural form, functional requirements and environmental performance. Tools used included:

— ESP+Suite, ARIA Suite, Dynamic Thermal Modelling (DTM)
— Computational Fluid Dynamics (CFD), TAS Suite, CARasol, Heliodon and Artificial Sky.

Natural ventilation using a plenum

The initial concept

The benefits of a well-designed atrium are widely acknowledged. At the Daimler Benz Building the atrium creates a sheltered buffer space of approximately 600m², which can be used all year round and reduces the heating demand of the facing offices. Potential overheating can be minimized by providing shading and sufficient ventilation.

The initial concept for the atrium was to use natural ventilation based upon a low-level opening at the front of the south-east atrium facade for air intake and high-level outlets at the top of the atrium driven by natural buoyancy. Shading devices were placed immediately below the atrium roof to reduce solar gain. However, DTM and CFD indicated that there would be an uneven air flow through the atrium resulting in poor ventilation into the adjacent offices.

The interim concept

The design was modified to introduce a plenum between the floor of levels 1 and 2. Air inlets of approximately 60m² were found to be the correct size. The inlets were distributed evenly along three sides of the building. This allowed air to flow smoothly into the atrium, and is reflected by the evenly distributed temperature profiles up the atrium. No air intake was made from the shopping mall side due to the risk of air contamination. The plenum also minimizes the risk of cold down draughts along the internal atrium facades. The hottest zone is located above the shading, away from the occupied areas. However, the proximity of the horizontal shading devices to the office levels 7 and 8 helped in terms of radiation exchange to the spaces.

The final concept

CFD analysis indicated that for a typical fifth-floor office the average standing head height temperature was in the region of 0.5°C above that when atrium roof shading was used. Therefore the ventilation criteria could be met with an increased performance for the atrium-facing office facades. As a consequence of removing the atrium roof shading it was necessary to improve the thermal performance of the atrium roof glazing to minimize overheating in the atrium in summer. The specified type of glass, Ipasol Natura, has a particularly favourable ratio between solar gain (34%) and daylight transmission (68%), and is double glazed to reduce condensation.

Further thermal analysis indicated that a heated single-glazed atrium entrance facade and double-glazed office facades would reduce condensation to an acceptable level. On the south-east entrance facade the use of an electrically heated laminated glass panel would avoid condensation. The atrium would be maintained at a minimum of 12°C with heating provided by fan coil units located within the plenum.

Atrium roof shading versus office shading

Four main aims led to the final concept of applying shading to the outside of the atrium-facing offices rather than to the atrium roof:

- to reduce visual cluster and obstruction at the top of the atrium;
- to optimize unobstructed sky views and daylighting to the atrium-facing offices, particularly at low levels;
- to improve accessibility and reduce both maintenance and the costs of the shading system;
- to provide occupants with the control of the shading systems.

The thermal modelling indicated that the optimum position of air outlets would be to distribute the openings evenly along the perimeter of the roof. The total outlet area approximately equalled the total inlet area of 60m². This allowed an even air flow outside the atrium-facing office facades. An additional opening of 3.3m² at the apex of the atrium roof relieved the hot air pockets and prevented them from spreading downwards. An additional 30m² of openings at the top of the roof were used for smoke extract.

Solar gains on facades

The facades of the building have been designed on a modular basis to meet summer-time over-heating criteria and optional comfort cooling criteria. Solar gains analysis, taking into account external obstructions, was carried out for all four facades. Thermal analysis was conducted to calculate the number of hours during the occupancy period when the internal temperature was likely to exceed 28°C. The additional target for the chilled ceiling load for optional cooling in the future was set at 66W/m². The building is sub-divided into different zones according to the internal office layout and the exercise was repeated with varying facade elements until the design criteria were met.

The outcome of the studies indicated that from an environmental perspective, both the external shading strategy and the integrated performance glass facade can satisfy the thermal performance criteria. The advantage of the latter system is the relatively simple maintenance and detailing, reduction in ventilation obstruction and the cluster of the facades. On balance, the integrated performance glass facade was the more favourable option. Depending on the orientation of the facade, various elements such as clear glass, performance glass, mid-pane blinds, internal blinds and opaque panels can be incorporated into the system.

Terracotta spandrel panel

Doubled glazed clear glass + Okasolar mid-pane blinds gz=0.25 u=2.12W/m2K

2700

800

400

700

Double glazed clear glass + external blinds gz=0.1 u=2.64W/m2K

1400

Raised access floor

Structural slab
Radiator panel

Slated ceiling to achieve 50%-70% exposed slab

700

Opaque panels u=0.43W/m2K

External Blinds

9.3 *Facade detail, Daimler
Benz Building, Berlin. Architects:
Richard Rogers Partnership.*

9.4 *Model showing view of
south-east facade of Daimler
Benz Building, Berlin. Architects:
Richard Rogers Partnership.*

A similar strategy was adopted for the atrium-facing office facades. Here, vertical external blinds are used on the upper levels where solar gain is problematic. The use of external blinds is reduced towards the lower levels while the amount of clear glass panels increases to admit more daylight.

South-east facade

This facade has conflicting criteria to reconcile, including views out over the park versus excessive solar gain and almost perpendicular incident angles due to unobstructed low-angle sun in the morning. Fins and overhangs would not be effective here. An initial thermal analysis indicated that the optimum device for this facade would be automatically controlled external retractable blinds. Overheating would be kept below 40 hours per annum. This, however, was rejected on grounds of the obscured view out, poor aesthetics and maintenance.

Further analysis examined the option of using a combination of opaque panels, mid-pane blinds, performance glass and internal blinds. The final proposal utilized performance glass with mid-pane blinds in the top and bottom panels and performance glass and internal blinds in the middle panel.

Typical facades

For the other three facades, a step-by-step analysis was used to examine the effect of opaque/translucent panels, external shading and performance glass. The three steps were:

- reducing the glazing area by using opaque and translucent glass where required; this lessened the number of hours exceeding 28°C, but was still unacceptable in many areas particularly on the upper two levels and the southern corners;
- adding vertical and horizontal external shading, daylight-controlled artificial lighting and exposed slab for night-time free cooling, which resulted in figures dropping by approximately 75%;
- replacing the external shading with performance glass; the number of hours exceeding 280°C reduced slightly, and in most cases the target could be met, apart from some areas on the top two floors where external retractable blinds will be used.

Natural ventilation in offices

In order to maintain thermal comfort in the office spaces, a more comprehensive study of the criteria as set out for the facade was undertaken. A detailed dynamic air-flow analysis was carried out for a typical externally aspected office module. This examined the viability of utilizing natural ventilation in an occupied office with still outside wind conditions for a summer scenario, using various window opening configurations. The analysis also assessed the overall natural ventilation efficiency. All studies were based on motorized top-openable windows and manually-openable bottom windows.

In general, the half-bay top-openable windows are motorized and can be manually over-ridden by the occupant during the normal occupancy period. Outside this period the top windows are controlled by a Building Energy Management System. Bottom-openable windows are located on every bay.

Slatted ceiling panels expose the slab for night-time free cooling. Motorized internal blinds are located at every half bay for street-facing offices only. Atrium-facing offices have internal blinds only where external vertical blinds are not needed. Artificial lighting is controlled by a photo-electric dimming system.

Heating to the offices is provided by radiators located at the street-side perimeter. There is provision for the installation

9.5 *Model showing view into atrium, Daimler Benz Building, Berlin. Architects: Richard Rogers Partnership.*

of chilled ceilings and mechanical ventilation. The air-handling units, which incorporate heating and cooling coils, can be connected to riser branch valves and heat output meters if required by the future tenants.

Daylighting

The atrium

Initial analysis using CARasol confirmed that by opening up the courtyard natural lighting levels within the atrium increased. To further reinforce the concept, the opening width of the south-east atrium facade increased with height. Further analysis demonstrated that in the summer the atrium received sunlight in the morning and early afternoon, and in the winter, in the morning only.

The daylight levels within the atrium suggested that planting would be most successful towards the front entrance and centre of the space. At entrance level, daylight level is sufficiently high (approximately 10–16%DF). The ratio of minimum to maximum levels is no more than 60%, with the darkest corner furthest away from the entrance. Direct glare from sunlight is limited to the morning hours only. On the whole, the daylight quality will enhance the atrium environment creating a comfortable space for the occupants.

The offices

Initial analysis established that the office depth and urban setting would be compatible with a good use of daylight. The basic daylight targets are as follows:

– to achieve 3% daylight factor (DF) 2m from the facade;
– to minimize daylight levels dropping below 2%;
– the front half of the room should be of an illuminance no greater than 5:1 compared to the back.

Modelling further suggested that external shading would reduce DF significantly and therefore external shading would have to be retractable. As facades become more obstructed high-level glazing plays an important role and hence the top panels at lower levels are primarily of clear glass or performance glass.

Conclusion

The building form was developed according to a set of environmental criteria such as daylight usage, passive solar gain and

Table 9.1 Daimler Benz Building, Berlin: main green features

– built form to optimize daylight, natural ventilation, solar control and views;
– ventilating facade complemented by night-time free cooling;
– use of atrium as thermal buffer and to induce natural ventilation assisted by air plenum;
– modular facade developed for solar shading with offices positioned to protect atrium from low sun;
– window configuration to maximize natural ventilation with minimum draught and good user comfort;
– facade costs 20% higher than usual (facade costs are 9% of total building cost) but help to reduce running costs by 60%; annual energy consumption predicted as 75kWh/m²;
– Embodies energy and CO_2 emission 30% less than typical office building.

natural ventilation, as well as aesthetic criteria. The design team believes that it has progressed the traditional atrium design by introducing a purpose-made air plenum zone with simple air inlets. This resulted in a near-external quality atrium with fully controllable and efficient natural ventilation.

Although the design first concentrated on the control of solar gain in summer in order to satisfy the thermal comfort criteria, components were subsequently selected to optimize the effective use of natural ventilation and daylight. Analysis of the final design indicates that annual energy consumed by the use of artificial lighting will be cut to approximately 35%, heating and cooling down to 30%, and thus CO_2 emission down to 35% when compared with a typical fully naturally ventilated office building in Berlin.

Furthermore, the embodied energy and CO_2 emission is approximately 30% less than that for a typical office building although the life cycle embodied energy is relatively high due to the choice of materials. The annual total energy consumption is approximately 75kWh/m², which is a quarter of that consumed by a typical office building. The building confirms that innovative approaches to design are essential if green buildings are to perform effectively at a personal, local and global level.

Steve Baker,
Peter Foggo
Associates

Leeds City Office Park

This office building project constructed in 1995 for British Gas Properties is, in addition to its low-energy strategy, of particular significance for three reasons. First, the building was and, at the time of writing, remains the only speculative commercial office building of this nature. Second, the building is constructed on a previously contaminated site close to Leeds city centre. Third, the mixed mode strategy for the building is a particular response to the urban location of the site and, for example, does not rely upon the opening of external windows to maintain comfort conditions within the office space.

Designed by Peter Foggo Associates, architects, engineers and quantity surveyors, the building is the first of several detached pavilions planned for the site. The brief from British Gas in 1992 was to provide 20 000m^2, subsequently increased to 50 000m^2, of B1 quality office space available to let at market rents, plus parking for cars, all set within a landscape framework that reflected sustainable principles and dealt effectively with the land contamination.

The key elements

The linear progression of ideas from earlier buildings by Peter Foggo Associates and Arup Associates (where many members of the practice had worked together as a team for more than 25 years) to this one contains consistent elements applied *en route* to other projects, notably Gateway House in Basingstoke constructed in 1982. These elements are:

- building elevations that respond to climatic demands according to aspect;
- mixed mode ventilation to promote energy efficiency;
- adaptable office space;
- minimizing fossil fuel use while maximizing the use of renewables;

10.1 *Daylight curve at window with and without sunscreen, Leeds City Office Park. Architects: Peter Foggo Associates.*

10.2 *Site plan, Leeds City Office Park. Architects: Peter Foggo Associates.*

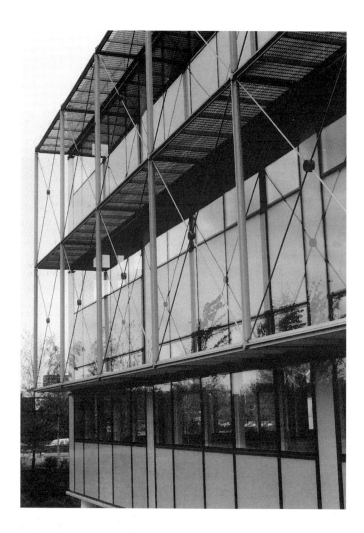

— structural design influenced by thermal capacity needs;
— architectonic expression of energy strategy.

Maximizing natural daylight

With the Leeds project we were keen to address artificial and natural lighting as imaginatively as possible. Since artificial lighting is the main element of bought-in energy consumption, the maximising of daylight penetration became an early priority. With daylighting, however, one problem is the differential levels between the edge and centre of the building with the tendency for lights to be left on even when working levels by daylight are adequate. When direct daylight and sunlight is allowed to enter offices at the edge of the building uncontrolled, the perception

of gloom elsewhere leads to lights being put on unnecessarily.

The answer at Leeds was to use solar shades at the perimeter of the building designed in such a way that they act as light shelves which, to a certain extent, deflect daylight back into the centre of the offices and, more importantly, reduce light levels at the perimeter. We designed the lighting shelves so that they doubled as maintenance walkways on the building facades. The use of steel and aluminium screens which combine solar shading, daylight shelves and access walkways, provides tectonic articulation of the mainly glazed facades.

Light, too, influenced the section of the building. The atrium was angled and stepped to optimize daylight penetration with materials selected for their light reflectivity. The atrium structure was kept as lightweight as possible to provide little obstruction to daylight penetration. The structure here, mainly painted steel and bleached timber, contrasts with the heavyweight concrete structure employed for thermal capacity reasons in the office wings.

In the plan the two angled wings were splayed to maximize solar gain in the naturally ventilated atrium. The effect is to open the heart of the building onto the sunny landscape park to the south and to close the building where traffic noise is greatest. The three-storey office wings and the atrium have different structural solutions, which serve different energy strategies. In the offices the concrete is left exposed as a troughed soffit for night-time radiant cooling and as an internal climate modifier during the day. In the atrium the stair towers project forward to enhance the experience of moving through the building with views of the parkland. A lightweight bridge at the front of the atrium joins together the two wings and provides secondary solar screening.

The atrium is larger than one would expect in a building of this scale. It has two main functions: energy conservation and as a social gathering space. On the latter point it serves as an area for informal business gatherings, to house small exhibitions and to provide the social focus an office building needs. The trees and dappled sunlight provide the office staff with an attractive, sheltered area to eat and drink. While the atrium serves an important function in terms of sustainable design, it is perhaps the equivalent of a small city square for the people employed in the building.

The three equal floors of office space providing 6900m² gross area are bisected by a core of staircases, wcs and main service risers. It encroaches into the 15m office floorplate where

10.4 *Long and cross section,
Leeds City Office Park.
Architects: Peter Foggo
Associates.*

least conflict with daylight and cross-ventilation occurs. A combination of shallow floorplates, angled wings, well-positioned cores and a large roof-glazed atrium provides a minimum daylight factor of 1-2%.[1]

The building's form and elevations reflect directly the energy strategy. The stepped and rising atrium section in particular enhances the natural stack effect of solar cooling within the atrium, providing up to ten air changes an hour in the summer.[2] The high level positioning of the plant room also responds to energy needs by allowing the return ducts of the displacement air system most effectively to vent the adjacent offices while drawing in clean air at high level. The solid to glass proportion of the atrium roof responds also to the balance between daylighting and internal comfort levels.

Central to the energy strategy is the use of heavy concrete structure left exposed as columns and troughed soffits in

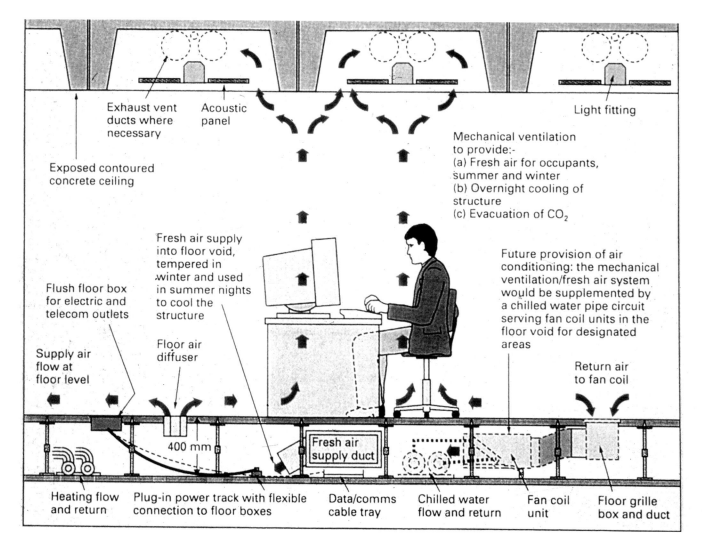

Exhaust vent ducts where necessary

Acoustic panel

Light fitting

Exposed contoured concrete ceiling

Mechanical ventilation to provide:-
(a) Fresh air for occupants, summer and winter
(b) Overnight cooling of structure
(c) Evacuation of CO_2

Fresh air supply into floor void, tempered in winter and used in summer nights to cool the structure

Future provision of air conditioning: the mechanical ventilation/fresh air system would be supplemented by a chilled water pipe circuit serving fan coil units in the floor void for designated areas

Flush floor box for electric and telecom outlets

Supply air flow at floor level

Floor air diffuser

Return air to fan coil

400 mm

Fresh air supply duct

Heating flow and return

Plug-in power track with flexible connection to floor boxes

Data/comms cable tray

Chilled water flow and return

Fan coil unit

Floor grille box and duct

the office wings in order to provide radiant cooling. For economy the primary beams do not span the full depth, but are supported at their midpoint on large round *in-situ* columns placed 7.5m from the facade. The exposed structure acts directly as a climate modifier while articulating the office areas into working bays. The exposed pre-cast ribs of the troughed soffit provide greater surface area than conventional beam and slab ceilings and hence maximize the radiant cooling effect of the structure.

Green solutions and cost restraints

The aim of creating a healthy, natural and attractive building within commercial office market cost constraints (both capital

10.7 *Upper area of atrium,*
Leeds City Office Park.
Architects: Peter Foggo
Associates.

10.8 *Open windows between*
atrium and office areas, Leeds
City Office Park. Architects:
Peter Foggo Associates.

and running costs) led inevitably to specific solutions. Balances had to be struck between mixed-mode ventilation and air-conditioning, between sealed and opening windows, between daylight gain and heat loss, and between high insulation levels and radiant cooling. British Gas Properties was keen that air-conditioning should not be ruled out and the design allows for subsequent upgrading if needed by tenants. However, the aim was one of encouraging green design within and, to a certain extent, beyond the limits of market preconceptions.

With openable windows arranged as three pairs per structural bay, a heat exchanger to pre-heat the incoming fresh air in winter, and large openings in the atrium roof to create a chimney for summer-time cooling, the building combines energy conservation with the provision of healthy working conditions. The building has a night vent system which blows air through the offices increasing the daytime air-change rate from 2.2 to 5.0 per hour.[3] Linked to a Building Management System (BMS) the arrangement ensures that the atrium roof windows are open when the night vent system is operating and that the fresh-air fans do not operate until the following afternoon in order to conserve cooling. Sophisticated modelling of the building by Halcrow Gilbert indicates that even in hot weather internal temperatures only exceed 25°C for a few hours a year.[4]

Predictions indicate that energy consumption will be about 30% of a comparable air-conditioned office building. In

Table 10.1 Savings in capital and running costs

Leeds City Office Park	Standard air-conditioned office
– shallow floorplate – opening windows – exposed concrete structure – displacement ventilation system – lighting control system linked to BMS – supplementary night-time ventilation – large wedge-shaped atrium – solar shading/daylight shelves	– deep floorplate – mechanical cooling – sealed envelope – large plant spaces
95% cost	100% cost

Savings in running cost

30%	100%

1993 the design was awarded a BREEAM rating of 'excellent' and received the highest score ever given at the time for office design. It will be monitored under the European Union's Thermie Programme (part of the Energy Comfort 2000 project involving eight other European buildings). Detailed monitoring suggests that solar energy provides 48% of the heat gains (68% in the cellular offices) making total gains of $75kW/m^2$. To ensure conditions remain acceptable in the offices, internal blinds under occupier control are needed on certain windows.[5] These would prevent excess solar gain and glare especially where direct sunlight enters offices via the atrium.

Conclusion

What is most significant is that the 70% saving in fuel bills has been achieved in a building slightly cheaper in capital cost terms than the norm for full air-conditioned offices.[6] The window element – an all-glass, structurally glazed cladding system developed specifically for the building – cost 20% more than conventional cladding. However, the raised floor needed to house the fan coils for the recirculated air did not add greatly to the building cost. The additional facade and structural costs were offset by savings in building plant needed for air-condi-

Table 10.2 Leeds City Office Park: main green features

– large stepped atrium to enhance stack effect ventilation;
– differential thermal capacity between offices and atrium to support energy conservation;
– use of natural materials;
– holistic approach to building design and landscape design;
– shallow floorplate and facade glazing to optimize daylight use;
– integral solar screens, daylight shelves and maintenance walkways on glazed facades;
– use of timber finishes from sustainable forest sources;
– reuse of contaminated inner-city site;
– service areas placed as acoustic screens towards busy perimeter roads;
– simple to operate and understand building management system.

10.10 *Entrance, Leeds City Office Park. Architects: Peter Foggo Associates.*

tioning. The lean and healthy Leeds City Office Park shows that low-energy design can be both cost effective and architecturally distinguished.

We approached the development from a holistic point of view. The design combines energy, environmental and ecological thinking both in the building and landscape elements. The close planting of trees to the facades, for instance, provides summertime solar screening as well as improving the air quality entering the building. Shade and natural scents from tree blossom outside complements the heavily planted atrium inside. Similarly, the lake formed as part of the landscape park is designed for wildlife as well as amenity. Reeds and

grass areas help to create a natural habitat where formerly there was contaminated industrial land.

References

1. *The Architects' Journal*, 12 October 1995, p. 37.
2. Ibid, p. 39.
3. Ibid, p. 40.
4. Building Services: *The CIBSE Journal*, November 1995, p. 45.
5. Ibid.
6. Ibid, p. 24.

William Gething,
Feilden Clegg
Architects

The Environmental Building:
The Building Research Establishment, Watford

The Building Research Establishment (BRE) has long been a champion of energy-efficient design and has in the past put theory to the test in its own buildings. The Low Energy Office, built in 1982 by the then Property Services Agency, showed what was possible at that time to reduce energy consumption to a level that set an extremely challenging target which remains creditable today: 120kWh/m²/ annum.

More recently these concerns have focused in the Energy Efficient Office of the Future (EOF) Project, a partnership between BRE and industry to 'identify new technologies and refinements in existing practice required to meet energy and environmental targets that will be in place in the early part of the next century, while satisfying the demands of owners and occupants'.

Demonstrating the potential of low-energy design

In 1995, the EOF Group produced a draft brief for office buildings, now published under the Best Practice Programme, which it sought to be tested in a series of real projects in a number of different types of location with a view to demonstrating the potential of low-energy environmental design to developers and building specifiers as an alternative to deep-plan, artificially-lit, air-conditioned building types.

At the time BRE was in the process of consolidating its estates by moving the Fire Research Station from Borehamwood to temporary accommodation at Garston pending the redevelopment of workshops at the centre of the site. This was seen as a prime opportunity to test the low-energy brief

11.2 *South elevation, The Environmental Building, BRE, Garston. Architects: Feilden Clegg.*

11.3 *Ground floor plan, The Environmental Building, BRE, Garston. Architects: Feilden Clegg.*

at Garston in what equated to a fairly typical business park setting with the further benefit of ongoing research and monitoring potential on the doorstep.

BRE appointed BWA Project Services to manage The Environmental Building project and set up a selection process that resulted in the appointment of a design team lead by Feilden Clegg Architects with Max Fordham and Partners as environmental consultants and Buro Happold as structural engineers. The building that has resulted is a genuinely collaborative effort – all consultants were involved from the earliest stages and were joined by the main contractor, John Sisk and Sons, during the production information stage, adding their construction expertise as part of a two-stage appointment using the NEC form of contract.

The brief

Intentionally open ended, the brief simply called for low-energy office space for 100 people that would be flexible and functional, and capable of providing both open plan and cellular spaces. This was to be coupled with high-quality seminar facilities to complement existing provision on campus. The Environmental Building was to be of a high architectural standard and was required to integrate an environmentally friendly approach with energy performance substantially better than existing designs (80kWh/m²/annum). It was required to obtain an 'Excellent' BREEAM rating and to avoid the use of air-conditioning.

The site of the original workshop buildings, which had been partially destroyed by fire, was at the core of the campus, close to seminar, lecture and meeting spaces in the original Mansion building, the Library Building and the previous Low Energy Office, and near to the campus social facilities. To the south was a car park, which was included in the site. A variety of building positions and configurations were explored. The final layout is an L-shaped building with a three-storey wing fronting a landscaped, car-free area to the south with a new parking area for 70 cars to the north.

The quiet pedestrian area formed provides a usable landscaped setting for both the new building and the other nearby 'public' buildings, and reduces noise and pollution on the predominantly windward side of the new building. The building itself is simply arranged with offices on three floors facing north/south separated from a stack of seminar spaces to the west by a glazed stair and entrance space. On the ground floor, a single-storey wing extends to the north to house a seminar space for 100 people, and exhibition and reception areas.

Ventilation

The relatively shallow office plan (13.5m) with fairly highly glazed facades exploits natural daylight and is well suited to cross ventilation through BMS (Building Management System) controlled windows at high level with manually openable windows at lower level. Occupants will be able to override automatic control of all aspects of their environment – a most important issue for any building, and one which a naturally ventilated building should be able to address more effectively than a sealed box. Cross ventilation is a natural choice for open-plan arrangements, but a degree of ingenuity is required to deal satisfactorily with cellular offices that normally interrupt a simple cross building air path. The approach taken here was to split the plan asymmetrically into a 4.5m deep zone on the north side of the building, better suited to cellular offices with single-sided ventilation, a circulation zone 1.8m wide, and a 7.5m deep zone on the south side best suited to open-plan workspace.

The wave floor

The southern zone was too deep for the given comfort criteria to be met by single-sided ventilation. To maintain cross ventilation of this area while avoiding acoustic problems between offices, a wave-form floor slab design was developed to incorporate ventilation routes that pass over the ceilings of cellular spaces. The high points of the wave have corresponding high level windows and daylight can thus penetrate deep into the plan. At the low points, large ducts are formed within the overall floor depth by bridging across the tops of the wave with precast concrete planks. Fire separation between storeys is at plank level so the ducts form part of the lower floor.

The wave-form floor structure is interrupted by the circulation zone which has a thin slab at the level of the planks over the floor ducts. This forms a crossover zone for air from the occupied spaces to pass into the ducts in the floor structure. The high level windows are at the same level as the floor zone and are arranged to coincide with the undulations in the slab to ventilate the ducts in the low points and the occupied

ELEVATION OF PRE-CAST BEAM

6.000

A

SSL87.800

SSL 87.200

A

CONTINUOUS 150MM WIDE FACE TO ALLOW FIXING OF VERTICAL DIVIDERS

LINE OF INSITU SLAB CAST OVER CORRIDOR BEYOND

TOE TO BEAM FOLLOWS LINE OF PRE-CAST CEILING

INSITU SLAB CAST UP TO SHADED AREA OF PRE-CAST BEAM

SECTION THROUGH SINUSOIDAL SLAB

IN SITU SLAB NIBS CAST TO PICK UP PRE-CAST PLANKS

75MM IN SITU SLAB CAST ONTO 75MM PRECAST SLAB UNIT

100MM SCREEDED FLOOR WITH UNDERFLOOR HEATING AND COOLING ON 50MM INSULATION

SCREED LINING TRAY

RAISED FLOOR SERVICE ZONE TO FLOOR ABOVE

B

50*75MM TRUNKING CHANNEL CAST IN WITH SINUSOIDAL PRECAST SLAB

VENTILATION PATH THROUGH SLAB TO FLOOR BELOW

OPENING TO VENTILATION CROSS-OVER ZONE BEYOND

VENTILATION PATH THROUGH SLAB TO FLOOR BELOW

OPENING TO VENTILATION CROSS-OVER ZONE BEYOND

VENTILATION PATH THROUGH SLAB TO FLOOR BELOW

75MM SINUSOIDAL PRE-CAST SLAB

PHILIPS T5 LUMINAIRE

20MM ELECTRICAL CONDUIT TO LIGHTS CAST IN-SITU WITH 75MMØ BESA BOX OVER TRUNKING CHANNEL AT HIGH POINT

B

LINE OF PRE-CAST BEAM ON COLUMN LINE BEYOND

REMOVABLE 75MM PRE-CAST CONCRETE PLANKS GROUTED IN TO PROVIDE SOUND ATTENUATION AND FIRE SEPARATION FLOOR TO FLOOR

SECTION THROUGH GROUND SLAB

C

100MM SCREEDED FLOOR WITH UNDERFLOOR HEATING AND COOLING ON 50MM INSULATION

SCREED LINING TRAY

RAISED FLOOR SERVICE ZONE TO FLOOR ABOVE

C

LINE OF SERVICE TRENCH TO CORRIDOR BEYOND

96

11.4 *Detail of wave floor, The
Environmental Building, BRE,
Garston. Architects: Feilden
Clegg.*

11.5 *Section through ventilation
stack, The Environmental
Building, BRE, Garston.
Architects: Feilden Clegg.*

spaces at the high points. The combination allows a number of possible air paths to suit a variety of planning arrangements and wind conditions. Air can pass, say, through the open-plan area, into the corridor zone and then into the ducts in the floor structure over a cellular office. Similarly, night-time cooling can be provided by opening high level windows on both sides of the building to allow air to pass directly through the floor ducts and/or across the office spaces or a combination of the two.

The wave form increases the spanning capacity of the slab, provides a beautiful ceiling to the office areas, and also increases the exposed surface of concrete and, therefore, available thermal mass for cooling. This is effectively further increased as, thanks to the ducts within the structure, both sides of the slab and the inner faces of the ducts are available to help to reduce peak temperatures. The floor spans between integral lattice beams at column lines, which allow partitions to be positioned against flat soffits.

While the design team was confident that the EOF brief could be met without the need for additional cooling, the opportunity was taken to test a further step of elaboration of the floor structure. The floors are divided into 1.5m strips of raised access floor, for flexible servicing, alternating with screeded areas which incorporate pipework that can be used for heating in winter (in combination with radiators for quick response) and cooling in summer. The cooling source is a new 70m deep bore hole into the chalk below BRE supplying water at approximately 12°C which is passed through a heat exchanger and returned to a second bore hole 20m deep. It is anticipated that this will reduce peak temperatures in the offices by about 2°C and the source is also used for the main seminar space where cooling in addition to ventilation was needed to meet comfort criteria.

Ventilation stacks

A building that uses cross ventilation as its principal ventilation strategy requires alternative measures to deal with hot, still summer conditions. The approach taken here was to incorporate ventilation stacks on the south facade of the building connected to the lower two floors. The stacks are positioned to draw air through the ducts in the floor structure, but there is also a gap between the south facade and the wave form slab that allows the stacks to drain off hot air from adjacent high points in the office spaces.

11.6 *Section through glazed facade showing Colt International motorized glass louvres, The Environmental Building, Garston. Architects: Feilden Clegg.*

Stack performance has been investigated by Cambridge Environmental Research using a Salt Bath model. This indicates that, under hot, still conditions, air will enter the building through high level windows into the cool slab ducts and drop into the centre of the plan, pass through the office spaces and exhaust via the stacks. To maximize their usefulness, the tops of the stacks are positioned clear of ridge and eaves eddy zones. They contain low resistance propeller fans (80W each) mounted at top-floor level. This gives them a predictable minimum performance if required and also means that they can be used for other ventilation scenarios such as to pull air through the floor ducts and across the office spaces on still nights.

The stacks are glazed using etched glass blocks, offering the opportunity for BRE to investigate whether there is a useful solar contribution to the stack effect here. The interior vents into the stacks are bottom-hung windows, also glazed with etched glass, allowing daylight to be admitted through the stacks themselves to contribute to the natural lighting of the office area. The stacks also fulfil a variety of functions in addition to ventilating the lower two floors in hot, still conditions:

— they provide shading against low-angle oblique sun from east and west;
— they provide a support structure for horizontal grilles at each floor level, which double as shading devices and as maintenance/cleaning access to windows and their motors;
— they provide a support structure for active external shading systems described below.

The top floor of the building differs from the lower levels to exploit the possibilities of daylighting and ventilation through the roof. As there was no requirement for the ceiling at this level to be constructed from non-combustible materials, a timber roof structure was adopted. The section is stepped along the line of the circulation zone with the south-facing roof rising to provide clerestorey light and cross ventilation over the northern cellular office zone. The stacks are not tall enough to provide additional useful ventilation to this level in still conditions, but the loftier section here generates its own stack effect. The roof is constructed using 75mm thick softwood structural decking spanning between purlins, which in turn bear on principals supported on steel columns. The combination of the thick decking with 200mm of mineral fibre insulation above is predicted to give adequate performance in terms of thermal mass and insulation.

Lighting and energy demand

Substantially glazed facades in combination with high ceilings and a relatively shallow plan depth mean that the need for artificial lighting and the consequent electrical load will be significantly reduced as compared with a conventional office building. However, as a corollary, the need to control glare and solar gain becomes correspondingly more important. In The Environmental Building these factors are controlled by using BMS-controlled external motorized glass louvres manufactured by Colt International, one of the EOF participating companies, used here for the first time in this country. These are 400mm wide, set about 1.2m from the facade and with the lowest blade on each floor at 1700mm above floor level. They are extremely slim when rotated to their horizontal position (10mm) but, being wide, are set well apart so that a reasonable view can be maintained when they are not required for shading. It is also possible to rotate the blades beyond the horizontal to a position where they can act as adjustable light shelves to reflect direct sunlight onto the ceiling deep into the office. Unlike fixed horizontal light shelves, they will have a minimal impact on the diffuse light from an overcast sky entering the building.

Initially, the intention had been to use fritted glass for the louvres to control solar gain while still allowing a good view out even when the blades were fully closed. Glare was to be dealt with separately by internal blinds. However, following input from BRE's daylighting research department and experimental work by the University of Westminster as part of a European Union Thermie grant, it was decided to try to deal with both aspects as far as possible by using 'fully fritted', i.e. translucent external glass louvres. The louvres are controlled by the BMS, but occupiers can override the automatic setting as they wish. The BMS will eventually reset them to an optimum position to avoid the common situation in which glare is controlled primarily by internal blinds, which, once drawn, tend to be left down and artificial lighting used more than necessary.

Control of daylight is mirrored in the careful regulation of artificial lighting (and thus a significant part of the building's electrical load) using the new high-efficiency T5 fluorescent lamps by Philips Electrical, another EOF Group member, linked to presence and light sensors, but with occupier override using infrared controllers. They provide general lighting at around 300 lux, which is supplemented by task lighting where and when required, and have an uplighting component to wash the wave-form ceiling to provide a balanced visual environment. Each of the lamps is separately addressable by the BMS to allow different light output levels to be assigned across the floor plan and thus take maximum advantage of daylight.

Electrical loads are further reduced by the incorporation of a bank of 50m^2 of thin film amorphous silicon photovoltaic cells on the south facade with a peak output of 3kW. The sloping south-facing roof of the building is designed to provide a surface for a further PV installation.

Recycling

While energy efficiency aspects of the project formed a major focus, the environmental aspects of the materials used to construct the building, and particularly the use of recycled materials, were also considered in some detail. The redundant buildings on the site were cleared with a view to maximum recycling. This was monitored by BRE which has estimated that 95% by weight was recycled, for example:

— brick and concrete was crushed on site and used as hardcore;
— roofing timber was sold to a company making pine furniture from recycled material;
— electrical fittings were given to local schools

Reuse of bricks from the workshops on the site was considered, but these had been laid in cement mortar and were not reclaimable. Even if this had been practicable, the process would have only yielded a small proportion of the total quantity required. A potential local source of bricks for the entire external skin was identified as work started on site (a nearby hospital awaiting demolition), however, at the last minute there was a hold up with the start of that project and second-hand bricks were sourced from a reclaimed building materials company near Cambridge. The process served to highlight both the possibilities of using large quantities of recycled brick and the drawbacks (cost, guarantee of supply, and brick size, etc.).

11.7 *Translucent glass louvres in operation, The Environmental Building, BRE, Garston. Architects: Feilden Clegg.*

11.8 *Elevation and part section of one bay of south facade, The Environmental Building, BRE, Garston. Architects: Feilden Clegg.*

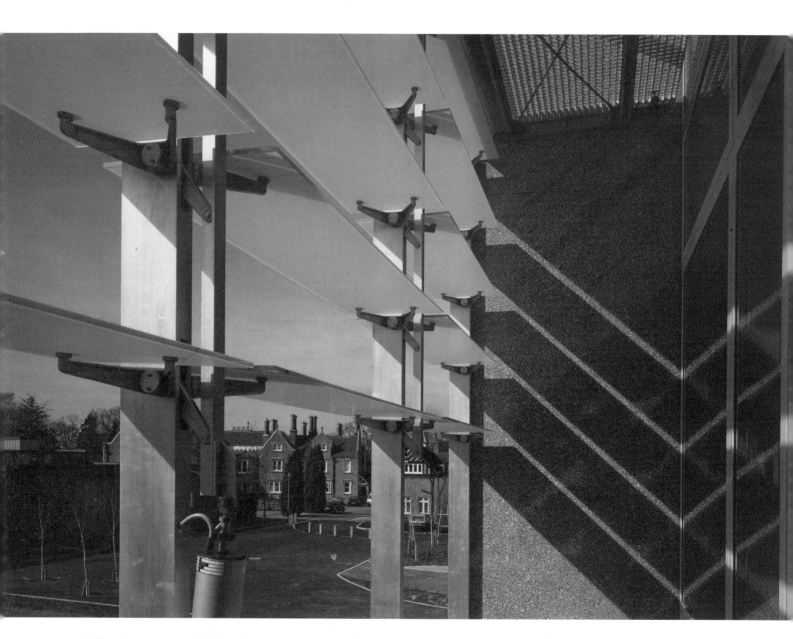

In The Environmental Building lime mortar was used for the internal cross walls of the entrance area (which do not take wind loading) to enable the bricks to be reclaimed once again. Valuable lessons were learnt for future projects on the structural consequences of using lime mortar.

Crushed concrete from a demolished concrete panel system building in London was used as concrete aggregate for the foundations, ground slab and much of the *in-situ* superstructure – another first in the UK. Again lessons were learnt on aspects of mix design, structural design liability, procurement (identifying potential sources, testing and stockpiling crushed material) and costs associated with using recycled aggregates.

Internally, in the reception and exhibition areas, wood-block flooring was reused from County Hall in London, a concurrent John Sisk building contract. Gyproc screeds, based on gypsum from power station waste, were used throughout the building.

11.9 *Section through office area showing integration of structure, ventilation and lighting, The Environmental Building, BRE, Garston. Architects: Feilden Clegg.*

SECTION A-A

SECTION B-B

11.10 South facade of The Environmental Building, BRE, Garston. Architects: Feilden Clegg.

Table 11.1 The Environmental Building: main green features

—   wave form, double ventilating floors;
—   facade ventilation stacks using glass blocks;
—   orientation and building planning to reduce solar gain;
—   highly-glazed facades to maximize daylight penetration;
—   manually openable windows with external motorized louvres;
—   combined external shading devices and maintenance decks;
—   lighting linked to sensors;
—   use of recycled construction materials;
—   photovoltaic electrical generation.

Architectural form

The building is undoubtedly unique, a strong architectural statement at the heart of BRE, but is founded on sound, widely applicable principles of environmental design that can be taken on by commercial developers. It optimizes natural ventilation, exploits daylighting, controls glare while still allowing a view out and, very importantly, allows occupants a high degree of control of all aspects of their environment. It incorporates a range of approaches to environmental control, the active south facade being the most evident, which have sufficient flexibility built into them to provide a fertile source of research projects for BRE for a number of years. Once in use it will be extensively monitored by both BRE and the University of Westminster, as part of the EU Thermie grant, which also covers the dissemination of the findings.

Conclusion

The Environmental Building seeks to demonstrate that responsible environmental design is a wider issue than simply hitting lower and lower energy consumption targets. In particular, it starts to illustrate the possibilities and difficulties of using recycled materials for a reasonable size commercial building and, in doing so, poses some interesting questions for clients, designers and the construction industry as a whole.

Energy consumption is easily measurable and thus the quest for ever lower energy consumption will continue with the probability that buildings may shortly be required to be net energy producers. However, the law of diminishing returns has already started to take effect. Energy is still so cheap that any savings in energy costs, as a proportion of total business turnover, are often so small as to be insignificant. On the other hand, as a result of much publicized research into the negative effects of a poor environment, the commercial world is starting to accept that the working environment has a marked effect on the performance of the people working in it.

We believe that future green buildings will be based on principles that fundamentally address many of the issues that have come to light from this research. They will offer good working environments in which people are able to work to the best of their ability, and have the added bonus of low energy consumption. What better demonstration that green buildings do, indeed, pay?

Chapter 12

David Turrent,
ECD Architects, and
Mel Barlex, Anglia
Polytechnic University

12.1 *Plan of Queen's Building,
Anglia Polytechnic University.
Architects: ECD Architects.*

Queen's Building, Anglia Polytechnic University, Chelmsford

The Learning Resource Centre (Queen's Building) at Anglia Polytechnic University in Chelmsford, Essex, is one of the first generation of interactive libraries to be built in Britain. Since the university already had an environmental policy when the design team was appointed it was natural that the building should be a model of best practice in energy efficiency. The site, a derelict former ball-bearing factory, signified the university's commitment to renewing the fabric of its home town.

The design stage

The building comprises 6000m² of library accommodation providing traditional bookshelf facilities, 700 reader spaces, a television studio and media production area, and seminar and catering facilities. The brief had three key features:

- to create a green building which would not cost more than other learning resource centres;
- to design a building which the university could use to enhance its reputation for good environmental practice and sympathetic urban renewal;
- to create a building from which lessons could be learned.

After some discussion the cost limit was set at £680/m² and in March 1993 the design team was assembled. It consisted of energy experts ECD as architects, and Ove Arup and Partners to provide structural and engineering design services. The technical team was assisted by the university's own project director Tim Mathews and Bucknall Austin, who provided cost advice.

The bones of the design evolved during a week-long workshop held at the beginning of the project. The design team spent the week with the client, evolving on the first day the energy strategy and producing by the end of the week

Table 12.1 Queen's Building, Anglia Polytechnic University: annual energy conservation kWh/m²

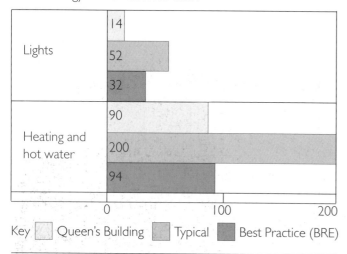

Lights	Queen's Building	14
	Typical	52
	Best Practice (BRE)	32
Heating and hot water	Queen's Building	90
	Typical	200
	Best Practice (BRE)	94

Scale: 0 — 100 — 200

Key: ☐ Queen's Building ▨ Typical ▦ Best Practice (BRE)

Source: Building Performance Research Unit, 1996.

the building footprint. As this took shape and was modified, it influenced other factors from lighting design to plan shape and external planting layout. The team sought a holistic approach that integrated the design input of the architect, engineer and landscape designer. By assembling the design team at the start of the project and by working closely with client representatives, the cross-fertilization essential in green design emerged without difficulty.

Finding an energy-efficient solution

Aware that electricity was the greatest slice of bought-in energy, the design team evolved a layout which maximized natural light and ventilation. By integrating the thermal and lighting analysis, and by relating the results of the synthesis to fundamental architectural and planning questions such as plan depth, building height, orientation and landscape design, we achieved what proved to be a remarkably energy-efficient solution.

Our strategy was based upon the principles of natural lighting, natural ventilation, use of thermal mass in the building for radiant cooling, and high-efficiency condensing gas boilers.

These decisions added nothing to the cost of the library over funding council norms, but allowed the building to achieve a 74% saving in energy use in the first year. Since it opened in 1995 the Queen's Building has been monitored under an EU Thermie Programme (Chapter 10, p.90) and results so far indicate an annual energy performance of 113 kW/m² as against the predicted 116 kW/m². Equated as a reduction in CO_2 emissions (the main greenhouse gas) the building achieves an 82% saving compared to an air-conditioned library. The Queen's Building uses about half the fossil fuel of a typical building, which is slightly better than the Best Practice guidelines of the Building Research Establishment (BRE). Remarkably these savings have been achieved at no additional capital cost.

Using the atria to maximum effect

The concept for the building is simple: two central atria, one at the north and one at the south, with library book stacks grouped around them (and hence contributing towards structural thermal capacity) and study spaces at the perimeter of the building to maximize daylight penetration. In cross section the building steps down from four to two storeys adding to the stack effect where the building is at its highest. The two atria are enclosed within the angled roof slope of the building, an arrangement which avoids turbulence and improves the look of the library.

The sectional profile of the atria was designed to deflect as much daylight into the building as possible. The angle of the balustrade and atrium walls at the top is splayed to bounce light into the lower areas and into adjoining library spaces. We also used fabric blinds in the atrium to diffuse daylight and screen glare.

The width, profile and height of the atria was chosen to maximize the stack effect in what is not a high building. Fresh air is drawn in around the perimeter of the building through window openings and low level vents, and exhausted through the atrium roofs. The currents of air are fan-assisted within the enclosed library study rooms. Floor to ceiling heights are fairly lofty (3.3m) in order to encourage thermal stratification. Since electric lighting is the main source of heat (about 60% of total gains) task lighting operated by the students at desk level is used rather than high levels of blanket ceiling lighting. Background lighting levels are 300 lux.

*12.2 Queen's Building, Anglia
Polytechnic University.
Architects: ECD Architects.*

Table 12.2 Queen's Building, Anglia Polytechnic University:
main green features

—   two atria to promote natural ventilation;
—   triple-glazed windows with twin light shelves;
—   lofty floor to ceiling heights;
—   natural materials and low toxicity in construction;
—   high structural thermal capacity;
—   use of tree planting to provide solar shade and enhance
    micro-climate;
—   energy performance better than BRE Best Practice, but
    at no extra cost.

Window operation

The design of windows is crucial to green buildings of any
type. Working with Samson Windows, we evolved a triple-
glazed window with a horizontal pivot-opening top section
and associated twin light shelves. As is normal these days, the
light shelves double up as solar shading on the south, west and
east elevations. Their main function is to prevent glare on the
VDUs around the perimeter, but they also reflect light onto
the ceiling. The opening of windows is operated automatically

since in a library there is little long-term investment by students in the quality of the working environment (unlike in
offices). The Building Energy Management System (BEMS)
controls not only the opening of windows but also the heating
system and fan speeds. Beneath each window there is an air
brick which brings fresh air into the building via the perimeter
heating system, giving a constant half an air change per hour.

Innovation within a budget

The Queen's Building is in many ways a prototype, and a variety
of design principles were married in its construction. We had
to evolve a relatively new type of building while also subjecting it
to recent thinking on environmental and energy strategy.
Though energy conservation was a prime objective, we were
also keen to look more broadly at the environmental performance of the building. We sought a design which would have a
small ecological footprint while positively enhancing both the
health and comfort of the building's users and the university's
reputation. Materials were selected for their low toxicity; the
finishes are mainly organic – stone, timber, natural fibre carpet-
ing. It seemed to us that the strategy of a low-energy, naturally
ventilated building required a complementary palette of natural
materials left in their untreated state wherever possible.

12.3 *View of atrium rising inconspicuously above library rooftop, Anglia Polytechnic University. Architects: ECD Architects.*

12.4 *Fabric blinds in upper part of atrium, Anglia Polytechnic University. Architects: ECD Architects.*

12.5 *Atrium, Anglia Polytechnic University. Architects: ECD Architects.*

Anglia Polytechnic University was keen that while being innovatory the Queen's Building was delivered on time and on budget, both of which were achieved. The new Learning Resources Centre has produced the energy savings predicted, and provides a pleasant and healthy environment in which to study and work. Of course, it is not perfect, but considering the scale of design risk entered into by the professional team and client alike, monitoring in the first two years confirms the appropriateness of the concepts.

Monitoring performance

Since the university was testing many new ideas in the Queen's Building it was decided to seek the reaction of users. The university's own Building Performance Research Unit (BPRU) conducted a user survey in the form of a questionnaire issued on ECD's behalf. The results of the 100 detailed responses confirmed that in the eyes of both students and staff the Queen's Building is a qualified success. Generally speaking the heating, cooling and daylight strategy work well in terms of user perceptions, although there is an acoustic problem of noise transfer from the open atria areas to the study spaces. It is clear that the thermal benefits of atria in buildings such as this can be negated by the transmission of noise.

Table 12.3 Queen's Building, Anglia Polytechnic University: perception of thermal comfort

Season	hot	warm	slightly warm	neutral	slightly cool	cool
Summer	6%	17%	37%	33%	5%	2%
Winter	6%	7%	49%	28%	7%	3%

Source: Building Performance Research Unit, 1996.

Table 12.4 Queen's Building, Anglia Polytechnic University: comfort symptoms

	Sleepiness	Stuffy nose	Headaches	Dry nose	Dry eyes
Summer	30%	10%	25%	9%	15%
Winter	40%	1%	15%	58%	12%

Source: Building Performance Research Unit, 1996.

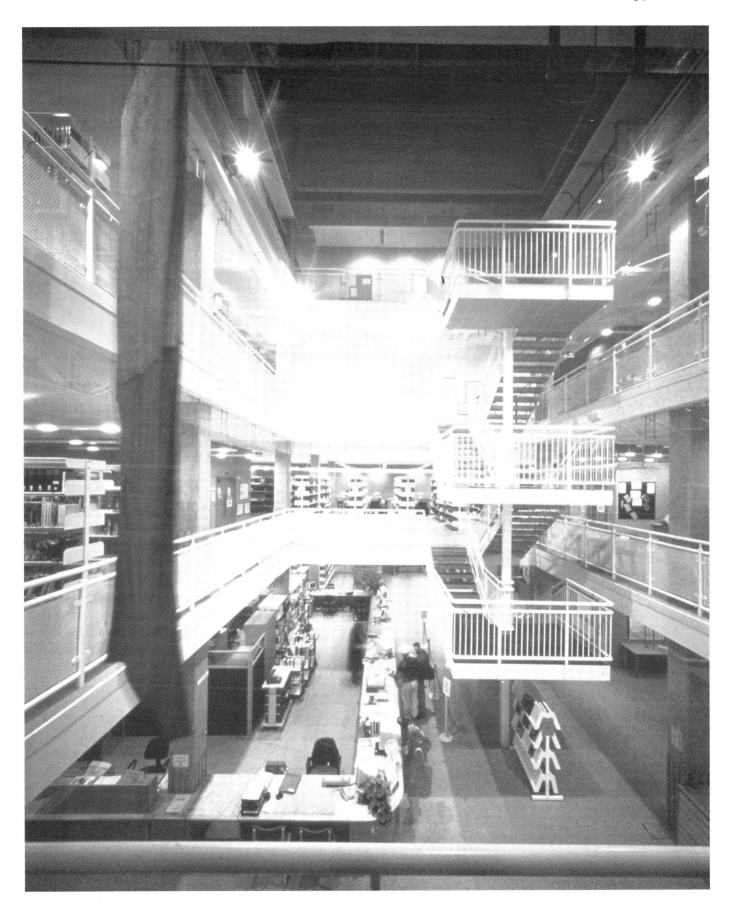

12.6 *Sketch by Ove Arup and Partners of window design, lighting and air currents, Anglia Polytechnic University. Architects: ECD Architects.*

VENTILATION OPENING AT HIGH LEVEL FOR MAIN AIR MOVEMENT. UNDER AUTOMATIC CONTROL FOR NIGHT COOLING, DAYTIME SUMMER

EXPOSED CONCRETE THERMAL MASS ABSORBS EXCESS HEAT

HIGH LEVEL VENTILATION REMOVES HEAT

DAYLIGHT

RADIANT COOLTH

BLINDS HEAT VENTED TO OUTSIDE

INNER PANES DOUBLE GLAZED LOW E ARGON FILLED.

REFLECTIVE BLINDS OCCUPANT ADJUSTABLE FOR GLARE.

VEGETATION ZONE ROUND BUILDING PROVIDES PRECOOLING SOFT MICRO CLIMATE.

LIGHT SHELF GEOMETRY AVOIDS GLARE ONTO STUDY AREAS. MIRROR TOP SHELVES

TASK LIGHTING

HEATING ALSO PRE-HEATS TRICKLE VENT

WINTER TRICKLE FRESH AIR WITH WIND SHIELD

Anglia Polytechnic University Learning Resource Centre

PERIMETER SERVICING ZONE

ARUP

In the summer the building was perceived as being consistently too warm and in the winter too dry; 33% of people found the library slightly too warm in summer and 29% in the winter, the remainder were happy except for experiencing headaches and drowsiness. The over-heating was largely the result of a sub-contractor who had over-ridden the routine for cooling to begin at 5.30am and forgotten to reset it, although even after this fault was rectified temperatures were still slightly too high. Evidence suggested that users were adapting their own clothes to suit the thermal environment. The problems of headaches and sleepiness could have been related to the air vents at the north gable not being opened in the early stages of the building's operation due to a short circuit resulting in the stack-effect air flows not occurring.

The following performance indicators are being monitored:

— monthly thermal electrical energy consumption;
— annual passive solar gain;
— measured overall building heat and loss coefficient;
— energy saving from the daylighting strategy;
— incidents of over and under heating;
— occupant responses;
— maintenance and implementation problems.

This data is being fed into the BEMS, which has dedicated software (developed by BPRU) to analyze the information and take appropriate action. The process has already highlighted weakness in the system and allowed fine tuning to occur. One effect of the data was to show that night-time purging of the structure was not working as planned, resulting in a higher ambient temperature than expected.

There is a great deal to learn from the Queen's Building – from its conception, construction and now from its users. One problem that did occur is that as a result of the design-and-build contract, a fair amount of contractor variation was permitted. The BEMS is useful, but did not provide the whole answer to the effective operation of the building from a user, energy and environmental, impact point of view. We had a great deal of information, but did not have the integrated intelligence to allow us to interpret it and take the necessary action. The building controls are sophisticated, the performance information gathered under the Thermie Programme comprehensive, but without a proper framework we could not refine the building management system to resolve some of the initial difficulties; however, the problem has subsequently been overcome.

It is clear that there is a mismatch between the assumptions in the BEMS and how the building was actually constructed, rather than designed. The principles upon which we decided to operate the building have proved robust enough, but the fine tuning essential in all prototypes has yet to occur. We are confident that when a few small changes have been made the slightly stuffy conditions and higher than expected temperatures will be rectified. The points currently being reviewed are:

— daylight redistribution from atria;
— reduction of energy use from lighting and catering;
— introduction of passive humidification;
— refinement of night-time cooling controls.

Conclusion

The Queen's Building is a challenge to many people's perception of a library. The sense of openness and energy efficiency depart from normal practice. In our view it is one of the roles of higher education to set an environmental example by developing new approaches to sustainable construction. Naturally, the building suffers from the teething problems of any prototype, but we needed to address both the physics of the building and the cultural understanding of environmental issues for everybody involved from client to contractor and student.

12.7 a, b *Pie chart by BPRU showing Thermal comfort in summer and winter, Anglia Polytechnic University. Architects: ECD Architects.*

a

b

Peter Yorke,
formerly University
of East Anglia, and
Richard Brearley,
John Miller and
Partners

Elizabeth Fry Building, University of East Anglia, Norwich

The University of East Anglia (UEA), founded in 1962, has a fine pedigree of Modern Movement buildings. The master-plan and many of the original buildings were designed by Sir Denys Lasdun. Sir Norman Foster designed the Sainsbury Centre for the Visual Arts in 1977, and more recently Rick Mather has added significantly to the ensemble. Other than Mather's contribution, however, most of the university's estate is marked by architectural rather than low-energy ambition. The most recent development, the Elizabeth Fry Building, is different: it seeks a marriage between high architectural art and low-impact environmental design.

Projecting an image

In the early 1990s the University of East Anglia learned through Mather's innovative approach to low-energy design that green architecture made sense financially and projected the right kind of image for a modern university. At Nelson Court and Constable Terrace, both designed by Mather to a brief that considered sustainable principles, the resulting buildings proved to be cost effective and, in their unusual design philosophy, attracted favourable publicity. Mather claimed, and monitoring subsequently confirmed, that the highly insulated residences would be heated mainly by the students' own body heat. The publicity was good for a university seeking to attract bright young students and helped to legitimise energy conservation and give it cachet on the campus.

Low-energy design principles

The brief for the Elizabeth Fry Building was written in 1992. It required the new building to be extremely good value for

13.1 *Site plan of the Elizabeth Fry Building at the University of East Anglia in the context of Nelson Court (right) and Constable Terrace (left). Architects: John Miller and Partners.*

money both in capital and running costs. Although the building was to demonstrate low-energy design principles, it was not to cost more than more orthodox approaches. This was the challenge for architects John Miller and Partners, who were appointed to prepare the design and competitive tender under the JCT 80 Contract.

The site for the Elizabeth Fry Building forms a courtyard with the wing of Constable Terrace residences and an earlier teaching building by John Miller and Partners. It is situated near the Sainsbury Centre in an area of the campus sheltered by trees to the west and Lasdun's megastructure of teaching areas and laboratories to the south and east.

Unlike the residences, which are occupied for 24 hours a day, the Elizabeth Fry Building was to be a conventional university teaching building inhabited during normal office hours. It was not, therefore, possible to exploit 'process' heat from students and equipment to the same degree. Calculations showed that the Elizabeth Fry Building needed two 24kW gas boilers (with a third as back-up), but not the full central heating systems normally encountered. Our target outlined in the leaflet Energy Efficiency in Buildings for Further and Higher Education (1992) was to get well below 190kWh/m^2, which is considered 'good practice', and approach the 'best practice' figure of 100kWh/m^2. In the event we achieved 119kWh/m^2, including not only heating, but also hot water, power and lighting.

13.2 *Detail of 'Termodeck' construction, Elizabeth Fry Building, University of East Anglia. Architects: John Miller and Partners.*

Finding an alternative to air-conditioning

The key to energy efficiency lies in the brief and the presence of an enlightened client willing to take risks. The university was particularly keen to avoid air-conditioning. Taking a long-term view of energy and building maintenance costs, and with concern for the health and wellbeing of those on campus, its policy was only to employ full air-conditioning in special areas such as the conservation room in the Sainsbury Centre and in certain laboratories. In the Elizabeth Fry Building even the enclosed lecture theatres avoid its use.

With the assistance of the energy consultants Fulcrum Engineering Partnership and Energy Advisory Associates, John Miller and Partners employed a novel form of construction known as 'Termodeck', which utilizes standard precast hollow core planks. These hollow structural members allow circulating air moved by pumps to moderate temperatures

(see Chapter 11 on BRE building). In winter warm air, heated by three domestic-sized boilers, is circulated through the building fabric: in summer night-time purging of the structure takes place using cool night air in contact with the ground. In both seasons the thermal capacity of the concrete structure has a moderating effect upon interior temperatures, assisted by air circulating through the hollow construction.

Maintaining high design standards

With a tradition on campus of providing high standards of architectural design, the new building had to achieve energy efficiency without compromise to the design expectations of the university. This double challenge led to many of the design decisions. It encouraged us to look to thermal mass as a means of giving thickness and architectural weight to the walls and contrasting this with deep cut expressive windows. It informed the organization of functions, with the largest occupancy

13.3 *Sectional isometric view,*
Elizabeth Fry Building,
University of East Anglia.
Architects: John Miller and
Partners.

rooms at the base. It lead also to the simple rectangular and linear form. The choice of colour and texture of the materials help to give meaning, in both a green and an architectural sense, to the parts of the building, which become visually lighter as they rise from the ground.

We sought an engineered solution to architectural design, but not a high-tech one. By sourcing materials locally and referring to conventional building techniques we were able to combine a form of contexturalism with more universal architectural aims. It was evident that with no additional capital cost available, the architecture, building services and structure would each have to contribute positively to energy performance. David Olivier, an energy adviser, helped to identify the critical requirements and evolve a simple sustainable energy strategy to suit.

When we analyzed the brief it became evident that the building could house at any one time a population of around 800 people in an internal floor area of about 3000m². With these numbers heat gains and adequate ventilation in the summer were identified as critical items which had to be addressed. Summer temperatures are particularly important to universities since this is the time of the year when students sit their examinations and precedent has established that poor environmental conditions are legitimate grounds for appeal for poor examination results

Planning the building

The site for the Elizabeth Fry Building was a narrow sloping strip edged to the north by trees, to the south by Mather's curving Constable Terrace and parking courtyard, and to the east by our earlier occupational and physiotherapy building. Orientation of the land suggested an east/west axis with the main student entrance to the south. The linear form of the building allows it to define a square with its neighbours and the choice of common materials and heights encourages a sense of

a

b

c

13.4 a, b, c *Lower ground, ground and second floor plans, Elizabeth Fry Building, University of East Anglia. Architects: John Miller and Partners.*

13.5 *South elevation with open arcade above ground-floor lecture theatres, Elizabeth Fry Building, University of East Anglia. Architects: John Miller and Partners.*

integrated and cohesive development in contrast with the openness of earlier parts of the UEA campus.

The planning of the building places the lecture theatres in a lower ground floor with single side access directly from a pedestrian walkway on the south side. Seminar and conference rooms for outside courses are situated on the upper ground floor with access from the north side, and a further two floors above are provided for more discrete departmental use. The arrangement of open arcade and solid concrete encased lecture theatres and conference seminar rooms on the south side allowed us to take advantage of the thermal capacity of the structure in contact with the ground while also providing solar shading. The heavy thermal load of 800 students, however, exceeded the ability of thermal mass alone to cool the building in the summer.

Energy-saving solutions

The employment of Termodeck in the construction assisted the cooling process. Widely used in Sweden, Termodeck is a proprietary system whereby the ventilation supply air is passed through precast hollow core concrete to adjust internal temperatures.[1] The system uses displacement ventilation with an air supply which brings air into direct contact with the ground via pipes placed under the ground floor slab. The result is a 'fresh-air feeling' and remarkably constant temperatures even under extreme external conditions.[2]

Two other factors led to low-energy consumption: a heavily insulated building envelope (U value 0.2W/m^2°C) with the avoidance of thermal bridging and highly airtight construction. The involvement of David Olivier and Fulcrum Engineering Partnership, the appointed building services engineers, at the detailed design stage, and co-operation with the contractor on site, helped to ensure air-tightness of one air-change per hour at 50Pa under the BRE fan pressurisation test.[3]

Cost margins did not permit raised floors and the exploitation of the thermal capacity of the structure prohibited suspended ceilings. As a result service ducts are limited in extent to the main central corridors. Also with no distributed radiator-based heating system, pipework is limited to vertically stacked wc cores. While the use of Termodeck added to cost, there was a considerable balance of benefit elsewhere.

Lighting and air extraction are combined in a system developed by Fulcrum Engineering Partnership. Air is extracted

over the light fittings to minimize heat build-up in cellular offices with corridors providing low pressure drop-return air paths.[4] Artificial lighting is confined to the perimeter of the rooms to expose the soffits, which act as light reflecting surfaces. Behind the light fittings are removable coved reflectors which provide cable ways for small power and data distribution.

The placement of lecture theatres and the use of exposed concrete structure meant that we had to maximize the surface contact between structure and air. The main structural frame of *in-situ* concrete with closely spaced perimeter columns supports a system of hollow pre-cast concrete floor and roof units. Below the raking ground-floor slab concrete chambers are constructed for the circulating ground cooled air. The integration of structural and services design is a notable feature of the building, especially the way fresh-air ventilation incorporates recycled energy from the heat exchanges. Since energy saving was our priority, each step in the heat exchange route was checked for its efficiency.

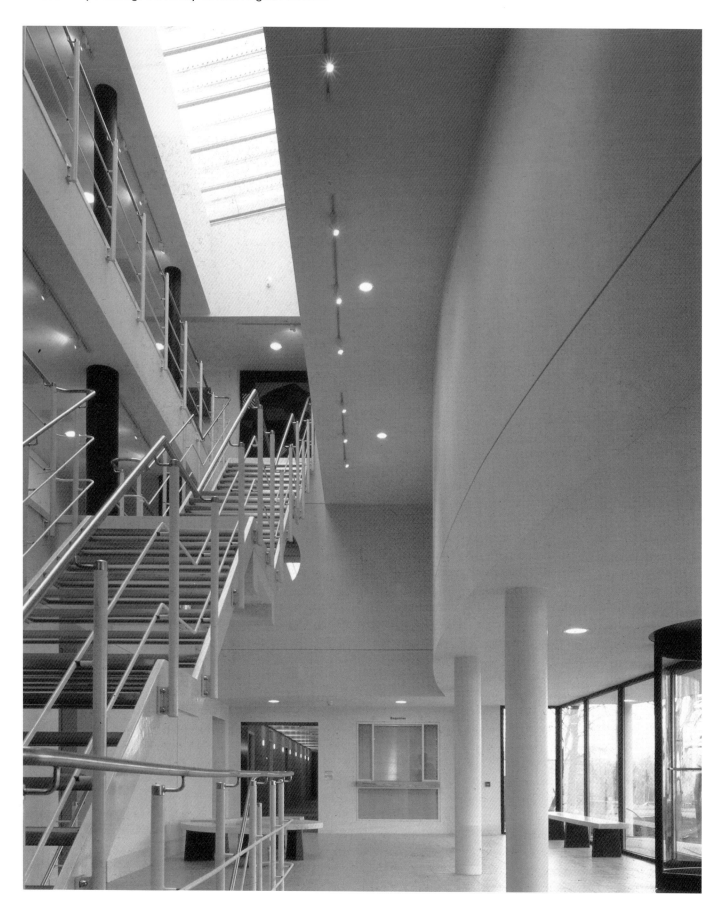

13.6 *Entrance hall at Elizabeth Fry Building, University of East Anglia. Note heavyweight construction and recessed windows. Architects: John Miller and Partners.*

13.7 *Translucent solar protection screens on south side of Elizabeth Fry Building, University of East Anglia. Architects: John Miller and Partners.*

Table 13.1 Elizabeth Fry Building, University of East Anglia: main green features

- orientation and building planning to reduce solar gain and maximise passive cooling;
- use of thermal capacity of concrete structure for cooling;
- use of Termodeck system of hollow construction for ventilation;
- use of ground temperature for cooling linked to Termodeck construction;
- shallow floor plan to maximize use of daylight;
- very high levels of insulation;
- high levels of structural air-tightness;
- integral lighting and ventilation design;
- triple glazing and integral solar shading on south elevation.

It is widely recognized that high thermal mass requires high insulation levels in the building envelope. At the Elizabeth Fry Building we employed 200mm full fill mineral fibre batts cavity insulation with plastic wall-ties to avoid thermal bridging, and 300mm mineral quilt at roof level. Windows are triple glazed with anti-sun coating and integral venetian blinds to control solar gain.

External solar protection is provided to windows on the south elevation where trees have also been planted close to the building for the same purpose. Rainwater from the building is collected into a holding tank, to irrigate the trees in summer. To comply with the client's need for low energy and healthy design we employed high-efficiency fluorescent lights with anti-flicker ballasts and generally place the control of the working environment directly in the hands of the user.

Conclusion

The Elizabeth Fry Building continues the UEA's well-publicized policy of procuring environmentally responsible, low-energy buildings. Like the slightly earlier buildings, the emphasis is upon a passive environmental response, good air-tightness, high levels of insulation, and active use of the thermal capacity of the

structure. Built at a cost of £812/m^2, the building provides considerable benefits in terms of energy bills at no great increase over university norms.

The solution is novel in some respects (especially the use of the Termodeck system) and is currently being monitored by the Building Research Establishment. Early results suggest that the predicted savings in energy costs are being met, and equally important, that the building is providing a satisfactory environment for learning while adding to the UEA's legacy of fine modern architecture.[5]

References

1. 'Sensitive addition to a campus', *The Architects' Journal*, 15 June 1995, p. 35. The building services account was prepared by Andy Ford of Fulcrum Engineering Partnership.
2. Ibid.
3. Ibid.
4. Ibid.
5. Personal communication with Professor John Tarrant, former Pro Vice Chancellor, University of East Anglia, at a meeting on 24 October 1996.

David Prichard,
MacCormac Jamieson
Prichard Architects
and **John Beatson,**
Cable and Wireless
Plc

Cable and Wireless College, Coventry

The Cable and Wireless College outside Coventry is a special kind of building with unusual environmental needs. Because of the large amount of telecommunications equipment used in training, the building has high heat loads and, since a plan depth of more than 40m was required in the teaching wings, the environmental and energy constraints on design were considerable.

The brief

The brief in 1993 from Cable and Wireless was for a green building, reflecting the company's demanding environmental policy as well as a tradition of naturally conditioned buildings as expressed in the Fiji branch headquarters building constructed about 100 years ago in Suva. This has big balconies, large open windows and a roof profile that encourages air flow. The new college was also to be environmentally friendly though for a vastly different climate and for an age when IT equipment represents a significant source of unwanted heat gains.

The site chosen for the new college is centrally located in England close to the University of Warwick and has good access for both public and private transport. The college operates as an autonomous business, providing short courses and residential training for Cable and Wireless and other telecommunication companies.

The client, architect (MacCormac Jamieson Prichard) and engineer (Ove Arup and Partners) collaborated at the outset to generate building forms that achieved the required environmental and energy standards. Building procurement from a green perspective meant that the environmental strategy for the new college had to dovetail into other areas of green operation, such as waste management, paper use, and employing suppliers with sound environmental credentials. This perspective influenced all aspects of the procurement of the building from the choice of site to the selection of consultants

14.1 *View of model showing teaching rooms in foreground, Cable and Wireless College, Coventry. Architects: MacCormac Jamieson Prichard.*

14.2 *Plan of Cable and Wireless College, Coventry, showing relationship between teaching wings (bottom), residences (top) and leisure pavilion (right). Architects: MacCormac Jamieson Prichard.*

and contractor. When you have a company committed to good environmental practice, the carrying out of building development provides an ideal opportunity to project a green image to clients and employees.

Commitment to biodiversity

The Cable and Wireless green building strategy does not stop at energy efficiency or waste disposal. It seeks to help to sustain biodiversity in both remote and urban situations by simple schemes such as building nesting boxes for the Bermudan Blue Bird into the walls of a new Earth Station on that island, and a development in Richmond providing roosting space for bats within the roof of the building. The need to develop new sustainable energy sources has not been neglected and pilot schemes for powering telephone switches by wind and solar power have been implemented in St Vincent and the Falklands.

The college at Coventry was not the only green building

14.3 *Detail of facade, Cable and Wireless College, Coventry. The wave-shaped roof is based upon the optional profile for natural ventilation. Architects: MacCormac Jamieson Prichard.*

14.3 *Detail of facade, Cable and Wireless College, Coventry. The wave-shaped roof is based upon the optional profile for natural ventilation. Architects: MacCormac Jamieson Prichard.*

14.4 *The rationale for the classroom profile, Cable and Wireless College, Coventry. Architects: MacCormac Jamieson Prichard.*

Hot layer forms at high level to be exhausted through openable glazing, driven by the buoyancy effect or cross ventilation forces.

Roof overhang and heavy construction protects from solar radiation.

Cool fresh air is drawn into the classroom by the forces generated by the buoyancy effect created within the classroom.

Room air temperature within +1°C of outside temperatures in summer.

Internal corridor.

Convector in floor void beneath glazing.

Radiator behind panelling adjacent to corridor.

HOT LAYER

under development by Cable and Wireless at the time. The John Cabot City Technology College in Bristol, designed by Feilden Clegg and engineered by Buro Happold, emphasized the use of natural daylight, natural ventilation and control of solar gain by user-operated external blinds and the integration of security with energy efficiency in the design of the facade. The green aspects of the Bristol College for 1000-plus pupils have been warmly welcomed by its users and were one of the reasons for the adoption by the college of a pilot 'global action plan' environmental scheme.

At the Cable and Wireless College at Coventry we sought a design solution which enhanced the company image, maximized the quality of the learning environment, and was energy efficient. The college consists of four building types, residential, teaching, administration and a leisure pavilion. The teaching wings (the subject of this case study) are arrays of 9m x 4.5m modules, which were derived from furniture layout studies for the different room uses. We had to be able to configure the space into a variety of sizes for lecture, seminar and laboratory rooms, and so for flexibility the dividing walls between the modules were non-load bearing and lightweight.

For reasons of adaptability the teaching wings are on one level and in the west wing there are four rows of modules creating a 43m-deep plan.

Environmental control

Going back to first principles, the design team sought to minimize heat loss in the winter and heat gain in the summer, and to reduce the use of mechanical plant and electric lighting. We also sought a solution that is simple in concept and operation. Implicit in the approach was the view that people learn better in an attractive, natural environment and that low-energy consumption is best achieved by straightforward measures such as orientation, built form, layout and understandable controls. Desk-top analysis suggested that a naturally ventilated college would use 50% less energy than a fully air-conditioned one. The precedent for the concept behind the teaching wings is the typical Victorian classroom with its height, large opening windows, perimeter radiators and high-level ventilation.

Our preference for simple low-tech solutions led us to analyze the three levels of environmental control:

14.5 *The wave-form roof profile and deeply set windows at the Cable and Wireless College, Coventry, reduces both glare and solar gain. Architects: MacCormac Jamieson Prichard.*

Table 14.1 Cable and Wireless College, Coventry: main green features

— high ceiling, wave-form roof profile based upon modelled air movement;
— natural ventilation for internal heat gains of up to $50kW/m^2$;
— chilled water recirculating fan coils in laboratories;
— natural and mechanical cooling systems used in complementary manner;
— high level of occupant control of working environment through blind and light switches;
— natural buoyancy ventilation using high level windows and low level air intake;
— differentiation of window area between south and north to prevent over-heating;
— extensive eaves oversail to provide solar shading.

— the building fabric is the primary climate moderator;
— the building services provide the basic stability;
— the personal 'trim' devices (e.g. opening windows) are the psychological safety valve.

The interaction between these levels leads to the building section which is the basis of the low-energy component of the design.

Wave-form roof

Architecturally, the most distinctive element of the college buildings is the wave-form of the roof, the precise profile of which evolved as we modelled air movement. The profile of the roof allows the building to achieve natural (i.e. non-mechanical) ventilation for internal heat gains of up to $50kW/m^2$. In some technical laboratories where gains are likely to exceed $50kW/m^2$ there are recirculating fan coil units served with chilled water from a 47kW chiller unit. Cooled air is supplied through the raised floor void to outlets below the heat-emitting equipment, thus neutralizing heat spill at source.

This results in the natural and mechanical cooling systems complementing each other. We reduced cooling to 47kW, which is very low for a $5000m^2$ building. In the teaching wings heating is provided by perimeter convector heaters served by a central plantroom, and within each classroom there is a pair of thermostatically controlled radiators which can be operated by the occupants.

Ventilation

The section of the roof allows independent ventilation for each room of the deep-plan building and there are controls within each room. Heat accumulates at high level and is convected out of the space and replaced by cooler air, which enters at low level. The section reflects the fact that natural buoyancy takes the heated stale air out through high-level windows and thus draws fresh air in at low level. The solution is elegant, reasonably cheap in capital cost, and efficient in terms of energy use.

A typical classroom has $2m^2$ of double-glazed window to the south and $8m^2$ facing north. Two-thirds of the north face is

14.6 *Cable and Wireless College, Coventry, with PowerGen Building in background. Architects: MacCormac Jamieson Prichard and Bennetts Associates respectively.*

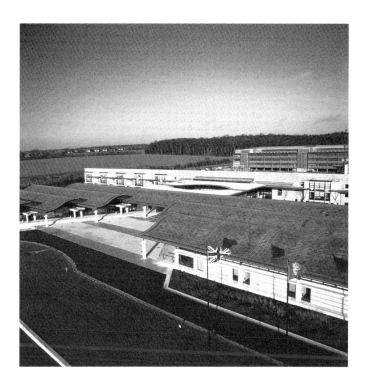

translucent to reduce glare. The roof eaves oversail the perimeter wall to provide solar screening for the exposed elevations. Additional glare control is provided by motorized diffusing roller blinds. A single row of switches by the door to each room activates blinds, two gangs of lights and opening windows, thus enabling independent control by the occupants. Corridors are lit by a combination of domed rooflights, wall glazing and halogen lamps.

By testing different classroom height and roof section profiles in the Department of Applied Mathematics and Theoretical Physics at the University of Cambridge (using the saline modelling technique) we were able to confirm the near linear relationship between air-change rates and internal heat gains. The models helped us to arrive at the optimum configuration for opening windows.

Conclusion

Major companies normally spend far more on personnel than buildings or energy. This means that staff comfort and satisfaction with the working environment is more important than energy savings, assuming that satisfaction leads to improved productivity. Simple, easily understood buildings such as this make sound assets if you take a medium to long-term view. Energy costs are currently low (though they may not remain so) so benefit to a company lies in having a building in which staff are happy, productive and encouraged to engage in creative intercourse. The simplicity of the Cable and Wireless building is important too – a typical college spends 32% of the building budget on mechanical and electrical services, but here the figure was half that in the teaching wings.

A Probe study has revealed that the building has not performed quite as well as was hoped. Probe is a post-occupancy research project managed by *Building Services Journal* and Halcrow Gilbert. It provides feedback on the actual performance of the building after a period of use. Perhaps in this case too many controls have been placed in the hands of untrained users resulting in overheating, underheating and high energy consumption for lighting. Like all innovative buildings there is a learning curve for occupants who are used to either air-conditioned space or the simple controls of a home. When staff and delegates have adjusted to the unusual design and its controls, and with a little education on blinds and lights, the building should perform much as predicted.

For Cable and Wireless the building emphasizes its commitment to innovation and sustainable business operations. After a period at the college delegates will return to often distant regions of the world with a greater understanding of the energy environment. That is another way in which 'green buildings pay' – they are part of the education needed for a more sustainable age.

Further reading

1. Probe 5: Cable and Wireless College, *Building Services Journal*, June 1996.
2. Where delegates go to have fun, *The Architects' Journal*, 11 August 1994, pp. 31–39.
3. Cable Talk, *Building Services Journal*, November 1993.
4. Facilities Economics, Bernard Williams Associates.
5. 'The Green Wave', *Arup Journal*, 1.1995.
6. 'Only Connect', *Architectural Review*, May 1994, pp. 24–31.
7. 'Wave Power', *Building*, 25 March 1994.
8. 'Hidden Assets', *The Times*, 22 March 1997.

Peter Smith,
Chairman RIBA
Environment and
Planning Committee,
1989–1997

Green buildings:
the long-term payoff

The case has been argued that environmentally advanced buildings make sense in both economic and social terms. If absenteeism drops, in some cases by up to 15%, it is possible to give this a monetary value. What is more difficult for accountants is to monetize the contentment factor. The physical environment is only one element in the equation – management style is equally important. However, an organization which has taken the trouble to commission an environmentally advanced building is likely to practice a management style that is compatible with the ethos of the building.

Global sustainability

There is another dimension to the 'green buildings pay' argument which refers to the infinitely more important balance sheet of global sustainability. There is much loose thinking on the subject of sustainability. Politicians are inclined to favour the Brundtland Commission definition of 1987 which states that we should pass on the planet to our children in no worse state than that in which we found it. This is a dubious objective since the present generation inherited a planet already on the global warming track. Even so, we are still far from meeting the Brundtland objective. A European Commission report (November 1996) declares that the European Union will only achieve a 5% cut in carbon dioxide emissions against 1990 levels by 2005. This is merely the level which could be expected from normal improvements in technology.

Returning to the Brundtland recommendation, it all depends whose children we are concerned with. For a child born in one of the small island states it is already too late. It seems that politicians from the industrialized countries have already tacitly agreed that these islands are a price worth paying in order to maintain the fossil fuel industry until well into the next century. Carbon dioxide is a gas that can live in the

15.1 *Twelve design principles for green offices and a prototype design by ECD Architects.*

The 'Green' Office Building
1 2   P r i n c i p l e s

- Shallow floor plans preferred
- Good levels of natural lighting
- Control system for artificial lighting
- Passive solar energy for heating
- Natural cross ventilation
- Night time evaporative cooling
- Efficient heating system
- Flexible auto / manual control systems
- Use of natural materials in finishes
- Avoidance of CFC's
- Use of sustainably managed hardwoods
- Avoidance of heavy metals

atmosphere for more than 100 years. Thus the momentum of the system has already signed the death warrant of these states. The International Panel on Climate Change (IPCC) states that we should be looking at a 60% reduction in carbon dioxide emissions as against 1990 levels as a matter of urgency in order to stabilize the climate. Against this yardstick, the 5% reduction by 2005 looks remarkably irresponsible.

The perils of climatic changes

There seems to be an unwritten agreement that the target date for reducing atmospheric carbon emissions to the recommended IPCC level is 2050. By then there will be at least a doubling of atmospheric carbon which means that substantial climate related damage is inevitable. Countries such as Bangladesh and Egypt will be devastated resulting in massive numbers of environmental refugees. Even Europe will pay a price. The Po valley in northern Italy will be a victim, as will large areas of eastern England. It seems the UK government is resigned to sacrificing large areas of grade one agricultural land in Lincolnshire and Cambridgeshire lying below the 5m contour to inundation and salination (50% of grade one agricultural land lies below the 5m contour).

The obvious solution would be to erect a barrage across The Wash. This would not only hold back the sea, it would also create an opportunity to generate substantial quantities of electricity through tidal rise and fall. It seems we would rather spend the kind of money involved in such a project on millennium celebrations. In contrast, Holland is already raising the height of its sea defences. There are, of course, the sceptics who say that the evidence so far does not conclusively prove that recorded climate variations fall outside the limits of natural causes. There are even those, like the Edmund Burke Foundation, who argue that the whole thing is a myth. They choose to ignore the fact that levels of atmospheric carbon are rising and the historic evidence shows a clear correlation between temperature and the level of carbon in the atmosphere. This was revealed by ice core samples and first reported in graph form in the journal *Nature* in 1990.

There is little doubt among the scientific community that increased concentrations of carbon dioxide in the atmosphere will warm the Earth. In the past quite small changes of global temperature have produced significant changes in climate. Since it is human activity which is responsible for most of this increase, the IPCC scientists in their 1995 Report were able to state:

15.2 *Correspondence between atmospheric carbon and temperature rise. Reproduced with permission from Nature, MacMillan Magazines Ltd.*

15.3 *Areas in the United Kingdom at risk from rises in sea level.*

'The balance of evidence suggests a discernible human influence on global climate.'

What is that evidence? Here there is only space to summarize some of the changes which have occurred over the last 100 years and which can, with confidence, be attributed to global warming:

— sea level has risen up to 250mm since 1860 and could rise by up to 1m by 2100.

— there is a marked increase in the incidence and severity of storms, which is causing grave concern within the reinsurance industry;

— receding polar ice is resulting in the rapid expansion of flora; Antarctic summers have lengthened by as much as 50% since the 1970s and new species of plants have appeared as glaciers have retreated;

— global mean surface air temperature has increased between 0.3 and 0.6°C since the late 19th century;

— seasonal shifts and changes in rainfall patterns are becoming increasingly pronounced;

— spring in the northern hemisphere is arriving one week earlier than 20 years ago;

— deserts are expanding;

— pests and pathogens are migrating to temperate latitudes;

— in Switzerland glaciers have retreated by up to 50%.

These are a sample of the physical changes that have a high probability of being the result of global warming. If the industrialized nations continue with their business-as-usual approach, we can expect to see an intensification of all the changes so far identified. However, the great unknown is the likely effect of feedback loops. Here are some examples:

— receding ice sheets expose tundra, releasing methane and carbon dioxide, at the same time absorbing solar radiation and reducing the area of ice reflecting solar radiation back to space, leading to greater melting, etc;

— oceans are the greatest single carbon sink; as they warm they become less efficient at absorbing carbon dioxide. The latest prediction in the journal *New Scientist* is that their carbon fixing capacity will decline by 50% as sea temperatures rise;

— a warmer atmosphere means greater evaporation with a consequent increase in cloud cover – IPCC scientists consider this will lead to a net increase in global warming;

— greater extremes of the hydrological cycle will mean, on the one hand, increased area of desert and, on the other, greater intensity of rain storms, which will increase run-off and the erosion of fertile land – both will lead to a contraction in carbon-fixing greenery;

15.4 *Solar House, Fraunhofer Institute for Solar Energy, Freiburg, Germany. Architect: D Holken.*

relatively rapid climate change will affect plants unable to adapt – particularly in danger are broad-leafed trees, which may not be able to migrate rapidly enough to appropriate climes (broad-leafed trees are a major carbon sink);

methane emissions from natural wetlands and rice paddy-fields increase as temperatures rise, adding to global warming.

Global warming

Why this excursion into the perils of global warming in a book devoted to architecture? The indications so far are that OECD governments are unlikely to agree to serious regulatory mechanisms to halt global warming in the short to medium term. This places extra responsibility on the shoulders of all concerned with technology which employs fossil fuels, principally

⌐ New Parliament Building, London. Note the exposed thermal mass, small window area and solar chimneys. Architects: Michael Hopkins and Partners.

vehicles and buildings. It is widely acknowledged that buildings account for at least 50% of carbon dioxide emissions in these countries. If the transport generated by buildings is added in, the percentage is significantly higher.

Of the 6 billion tonnes of carbon currently deposited in the atmosphere due to human activity, about 4.5 tonnes attributable to the industrialized countries of which half is due to buildings. The technology exists to reduce the energy consumption of buildings by an overall average of 60%. If this were to be realized across the board it would result in a saving of 1.35 billion tonnes of carbon. Obviously this is not achievable in the short term, but it does highlight the fact that the design of new buildings and the retrofitting of existing properties can have a significant impact on global warming. Architects and engineers could contribute to a sustainable planet to an extent comparable to the aims of international agreements such as those reached at the Rio Summit. That is why it is important for all concerned with the built environment to understand the scale of the problem.

Towards sustainable buildings

The first jolt to our energy complacency came with the oil shocks of the 1970s. Energy conservation assumed impor-

tance in order to conserve stocks of fossil fuels. This introduced the first phase of energy conscious buildings.

The second phase followed the realization that emissions of carbon dioxide are forcing up the greenhouse effect leading to a measurable warming of the planet. The buildings in this book are at the leading edge of this phase.

The next generation of buildings are likely to emerge in response to a number of catastrophic consequences of global warming. Following the success of passive buildings in coping with the extreme temperatures of the 1995 summer, the scepticism which generally attached to passively ventilated buildings took a jolt. Another assumption that has been undermined is that passive buildings rely for cooling on opening windows. The New Parliament Building designed by Michael Hopkins and Partners is demonstrating that, provided the exposed thermal mass and radiated cooling is sufficiently large, there is no need for opening windows, especially when the external temperature is high. Heat flow into the thermal mass from office spaces can realize peak indoor temperatures up to 8°C cooler than the external temperature.

On-site electricity generation will become increasingly attractive as photovoltaic (PV) cells become more efficient and less costly. In the UK stand-alone generation with a link to the grid would become much more economically attractive if the buying-in rates imposed by the power companies were closer to the market price. At present private generators receive about one-fifth the unit price charged to domestic consumers. Compact multiple wind turbines and small-scale hydro will also become more popular where conditions allow.

Renewable energy is becoming even more viable when associated with efficient means of energy storage. Battery technology has advanced little over the past century and so offers only short-term bridging power. The use of PV cells to create hydrogen via an electrolyzer is another way of creating electricity storage since the hydrogen can be used to operate a fuel cell. The Solar House in Freiburg, Germany, is an example of the use of this technology.

Already there are commercial buildings which feature the seasonal storage of solar energy in the form of heat in insulated compartments containing a high thermal mass material: bricks, concrete blocks, even water. Storage for both heating and cooling is possible using a phase change material and the latent heat of fusion to provide high density storage. A system in common use employs small storage vessels containing eutectic

15.6 *Photovoltaic (PV) cells used to create hydrogen via an electrolyzer at the Solar House, Fraunhofer Institute for Solar Energy, Freiburg, Germany. Architect: D Holken.*

salts and hydrates. This is ideal where there is a cyclic demand for both cooling and heating, flattening the peaks and troughs of demand.

These are some of the technologies which have arisen in response to the third phase in the greening of architecture. The final phase will be realized after some significant advances in technology.

The autonomous building

At present PV cells achieve at best 17% efficiency. Within the next two decades this is expected to rise to 50%, with hydrophobic glass inhibiting the accumulation of dirt on their surface. Electricity storage will be transformed when superconductivity is possible at near room temperature. Massive amounts of electricity will be able to be stored in a ring of superconducting cables with no power loss and tapped to suit demand. Every major building may have its electricity reservoir, suitably constructed to be secure.

Buildings often benefit from technological developments driven by other things, like the way the pace of battery technology is being impelled by lap-top computers. Vehicle technology is behind the latest development in hydrogen storage. This concerns the capacity of nanofibres of graphite to store hydrogen. Researchers at the North-eastern University in Boston, Massachusetts, have produced a graphite storage material that can store up to three times its own weight in hydrogen under pressure at room temperature. This creates the prospect of producing sealed cartridges, which are pressurized to 40 atmospheres to keep the hydrogen molecules in place. The gas is released by gradually reducing the pressure. The cartridges are portable and, it is claimed, capable of powering an electric car for 8000km. The application for buildings down to the domestic scale is obvious.

Flywheel technology is making a breakthrough because of its application to space technology. Flywheels cannot only store electricity as a satellite passes across the sun, they can also act as stabilizers. New materials are able to stand centrifugal forces generated by 55 000rpm. Micro-flywheels no more than 1.5cm across are being developed to spin at 90 000rpm. The energy density of these advanced flywheels is about 44Wh/kg. However, they are being challenged by a flywheel developed in the University of Maryland, which can reach 600 000rpm with an energy density of 250Wh/kg. The relevance to energy storage in buildings is obvious.

Other advances include new polymers, for example, piezoelectric polymer modules which could be another source of electricity, given the right conditions. Similarly, waste products will be totally 'digested' on site possibly providing another source of energy. Buildings may also have their own stand alone hydrological cycle.

Green building of the future: the architect's challenge

By the middle of the next century it is possible to envisage buildings that make no demands on the environment apart from their embodied energy. Indeed, they may well be net exporters to the grid of clean electricity. They will be long-life structures, capable of being dismantled at the end of their life and perhaps 90% recyclable.

Architects and engineers are in a position to demonstrate how a fundamental change of attitude to the practice of their vocation can have a measurable impact on the destiny of the planet. It is up to them to set the example which others may feel moved to follow. The environmental problems we face provide the single greatest challenge for building design into the next century.

Index